One Pan,
Whole Family

One Pan, Whole Family

MORE THAN 70 COMPLETE
WEEKNIGHT MEALS

Carla Snyder

PHOTOGRAPHS BY **Colin Price**

CHRONICLE BOOKS

SAN FRANCISCO

Text copyright © 2018 by **Carla Snyder.**

Photographs copyright © 2018 by **Colin Price.**

Library of Congress Cataloging-in-Publication Data

Names: Snyder, Carla, author.
Title: One pan, whole family / Carla Snyder ;
    photographs by Colin Price.
Description: San Francisco : Chronicle Books, [2018]
    | Includes index.
Identifiers: LCCN 2017054584 | ISBN 9781452168708
    (pbk. : alk. paper)
Subjects: LCSH: Cooking. | Families—Nutrition. |
    One-dish meals. | LCGFT: Cookbooks.
Classification: LCC TX714 .S6113 2018 | DDC
    641.82—dc23 LC record available at
    https://lccn.loc.gov/2017054584

Manufactured in China.

Designed and illustrated by **Cat Grishaver.**
Food styling by **Emily Caneer.**
Prop styling by **Glenn Jenkins.**

10 9 8 7 6 5 4 3 2 1

Chronicle books and gifts are available at special quantity discounts to corporations, professional associations, literacy programs, and other organiza-tions. For details and discount information, please contact our premiums department at corporate sales@chroniclebooks.com or at 1-800-759-0190.

Chronicle Books LLC
680 Second Street
San Francisco, California 94107
www.chroniclebooks.com

Dedication

TO MY EATERS IN TRAINING, THE GRANDBABES: KYLEY, EMMA, CHARLIE, AND THE NEW ONE ON THE WAY! YOUR APPETITE FOR LIFE INSPIRES ME EVERY DAY.

contents

For many of us, the end of the workday is really just the beginning of another stretch of work. On the drive home, our minds are busy with thoughts of ferrying kids to activities, homework, household chores, and the big job of the night, making dinner for the family. I can't help you with the carpool to swimming practice or folding your laundry, but my last two books, *One Pan, Two Plates* and *One Pan, Two Plates: Vegetarian Suppers*, have given thousands the tools and recipes to prepare made-from-scratch meals in minimal time and with less cleanup. While those books are scaled for two people, families have clamored for one-pan meals for four to six people as well.

They need a cookbook full of interesting, healthy recipes, ready in 45 minutes or less, with simple directions and only one pan to clean up after dinner is done. Imagine reducing the time spent on this nightly chore and turning it into more quality time spent relaxing with your family.

That's where *One Pan, Whole Family* comes in. All the dishes in the book are complete, made-from-scratch meals, ready to eat in less time than it takes to order and pick up take-out. These are not boring casseroles, but dishes good enough to serve for company, like Chicken and Swiss Chard in Cider-Cream Sauce, Rosemary Pork Tenderloin with Carrots and Fig-Yogurt Sauce, and Prosciutto-Roasted Ruby Trout with Zucchini and Butter Beans. I've taken what I learned from my thirty-plus years as a cooking school teacher, caterer, artisan baker, and recipe developer to combine ingredients that cook deliciously together to create a complete meal in one pan.

It's very simple. Let's look at Pork Chops with Sweet Potatoes and Apple Glaze. It all starts with a hot, hot oven so it cooks quickly. Sweet potatoes and pears are chopped and arranged on a sheet pan to roast for 15 minutes. Pork chops are salted and peppered and added to the pan, which goes back into the oven for another 15 minutes. Apple jelly is dolloped onto the chops, the whole pan is cooked for another 5 minutes so the jelly becomes a sweet glaze, and dinner is done. It's a fresh, healthful meal that kids and adults alike will enjoy, ready to eat in under 45 minutes—and you may not even have to clean the sheet pan if you line it with foil.

I know how much time it takes to plan meals. That's why *One Pan, Whole Family* has done that chore for you. All the recipes are a complete meal with no extra thought or planning involved. Once you pick a recipe, that's it. Dinner is almost done.

Whether you are a young family just starting out or a family with teenagers getting ready to fly the nest, the recipes in this book are both kid-friendly and adventuresome. After all, dinner should be interesting, right? I've raised a family myself and now have grandchildren, so I know that families don't always respond to what's on the plate in the same way. But who has the time to make separate meals for the kids? So I've developed these recipes with an eye to children's tastes along with Extra-Hungry Kids options for those nights when you might like a little more food on the plate. Because I've kept the recipes on the tame side for the kids, each recipe also includes an Adult Taste Buds option where you can spice it up or create a more adult-flavored option for the adult portions. That way one recipe has the power to make everyone at the table happy—not a small thing!

Most of the cooking in *One Pan, Whole Family* is done in a 12-in [30.5-cm] heavy skillet with a lid but I've also employed a 4-qt [3.8-L] saucepan for soups and stews and a rimmed sheet pan for fix-it-and-forget-it oven roasting. None of this equipment needs to be expensive and I urge you to invest (if you haven't already) in a 12-in [30.5-cm] cast-iron skillet, a sharp santoku-style knife, and a 20-in [50-cm] dishwasher-safe cutting board to make the cooking process more successful and enjoyable. The heavy-gauge pan allows you to cook over higher heat, cooking faster and more efficiently, and also helps in browning meats and vegetables—this translates to more flavor. The larger knife actually works more efficiently than a small paring knife, and with practice you'll be cutting vegetables faster and with less effort. The sheet pan provides a large surface for roasting vegetables and proteins in one layer, resulting in faster cooking and more browning and flavor.

This is a low-tech cookbook; no food processors, blenders, mixers, or special gadgets are necessary, though a Microplane for zesting and an inexpensive mandoline for extra-thin slicing are handy and worth the price and space in your kitchen.

I've set up the recipes in an easy-to-follow format, informing you clearly every step of the way, streamlining the process and creating efficiencies of time and work. For example, I explain in each recipe exactly how to cut the vegetables so that they cook in the prescribed times. Sometimes I may direct you back to the cutting board to prepare ingredients while part of the recipe bubbles away on the stove. I have a saying that everyone should be a caterer for a week. That way you learn efficiencies and how to make the best use of your time. This book reflects those efficiencies for the home cook.

The book begins with a chapter called "Veggie Good." These recipes are vegetarian and I've included them for vegetarians, people who cook for vegetarians, and people who simply want to embrace a diet that has more wholesome, delicious vegetables and grains and less meat. With so many diets in vogue, whether vegetarian, vegan, paleo, or gluten-free, to name a few, it can be challenging to get a meal on the table that suits everyone's needs. This chapter can serve as a bridge, as most of its recipes will work as a main dish for some and a delicious side to quickly grilled chicken or fish for others. Recipes like Parmesan-Crusted Cauliflower Steaks with Farro, Root Vegetable Quinoa Bowl with Tahini, and Cheesy Angel Hair Pasta with Asparagus and Basil are hearty meals showcasing fresh vegetables and are sure to please even the pickiest palates.

"Winner, Winner, Chicken Dinner" includes the kind of classic chicken and turkey dinner staples that have nourished hungry families for decades, but with a twist. Cuban-Style Chicken Fricassee takes a simple American staple and enhances it with the flavors of the tropics by way of citrus in a sweet-and-sour tomatoey sauce with potatoes, peppers, and raisins. There's also Chicken Pot Pie on the Fly and Chicken Fingers with Smashed Potatoes and Mexican Dip for those with less adventurous palates, not to mention Chicken Soup with Leeks and Wide Noodles, a family-pleasing soup that even grandma would be proud to serve.

"Let's Eat Meat" features beef, pork, and sausage, including must-haves like Beef Fajitas with Guacamole; Open-Faced Super Burgers with Cheddar, Mushrooms, and Onion; and an ingenious Stovetop Lasagna with Spinach that probably deserves an award for its flavor and ease. For extra nutrition, I've even sneaked grated carrots into the Barbecue Meat Loaf Patties with Herbed Smashed Potatoes and Green Beans. What mom doesn't like that?

"Go Fish" is a seafood chapter brimming with healthy dinner options, such as Asian-Style Fish Tacos with Wilted Cabbage Slaw; Prosciutto-Roasted Ruby Trout with Zucchini and Butter Beans; and Bow Ties with Shrimp, Spinach, and Feta. Light and lean, fish dinners cook in a flash, and when paired with fresh vegetables, there's nothing that's better tasting or better for you. Fish can sometimes be a tough sell for kids, so I've taken special care to incorporate flavors appealing to children, such as Shrimp Pizza with Pineapple and Spinach and Coconut-Crusted Tilapia with Broccoli and Sweet Chili Sauce. From ruby trout to halibut and haddock to snapper, there's a fish dish just waiting to become your family's new favorite.

This book is my love letter to my kids and to anyone, young or old, who would like to get back to the basics of feeding their families more freshly cooked meals with less processed ingredients. As it turns out, it's actually NOT that hard for families to get a healthy meal on the table every night. With a couple of useful skills under your belt and some go-to recipes, making dinner is quick and easy and your whole family will love it. My mission as a cooking school teacher has always been to help my students learn the skills they need to operate efficiently and enjoyably in the quest to feed themselves and others. I hope this book helps reset the game by offering an easy-to-follow plan to feed hungry families in a healthy and less stressful way.

So, here you go, kids. Cook away.

tips to help you cook with speed and success

The mission of *One Pan, Whole Family* is to make cooking less stressful and more enjoyable and delicious. To that end, I've listed some tips here to make the cooking process more successful. In the recipes, I direct you from the preparation of ingredients through to the finished meal, so there's very little for you to analyze. I've thought out the entire process so you don't have to. The goal is to have you cooking like the pros with efficiency, less stress, and more fun.

Read the recipe completely. When teaching a hands-on cooking class, the first thing I tell my students is to read the entire recipe before beginning to cook. That way you won't have any surprises and you'll be less likely to make mistakes.

Preheat the oven. Also, put a pot on to boil (if you need it) as soon as you find out that you need it in the recipe. That way it'll be ready when you are.

Mise en place. That's when you pull the ingredients from the fridge and pantry and arrange them on the counter. This makes it easier to prep the recipe and ascertain that you have all the ingredients on hand. Running to the store to pick up a missing ingredient should be avoided at all costs.

Buy a heavy ovenproof skillet. The recipes in all my books require a heavy 12-in [30.5-cm] skillet with an ovenproof handle and lid because I often direct you to start cooking on the stovetop but then transfer the pan to the oven to finish cooking. Serious cooks know a heavy skillet will allow you to use higher heat (which cooks faster), resulting in a better sear and more nicely browned exterior than most lightweight cookware. A cast-iron pan is inexpensive and will last you a lifetime (and your children's lifetime after that).

Buy a large, deep saucepan. A 4-qt [3.8-L] saucepan is a very useful piece of cookware. You'll use it whenever you require a deeper vessel to cook things like pasta, soups, and stews. It's the second-most-used pan in my house and it will be in your home as well.

A heavy sheet pan will change your life. A sheet pan isn't a cookie sheet (though it can be used as one). It has sides and the dimensions are usually 18 by 13 in [46 by 33 cm]. Don't buy the ones sold at the grocery store, because they will torque and twist in the oven as they heat up. Instead, opt for the heavier sheet pans sold in cookware stores. They'll hold up longer and perform at a much higher level. Use nonstick foil when lining the pan and nothing will stick.

A chef's knife will make you a better cook. A quality knife is the best investment you can make. Cutting up vegetables with a dull knife is a chore, but a sharp knife makes cutting a pile of vegetables, if not fun, at least less work. I recommend a 7-in [17-cm] or 8-in [20-cm] santoku, which is a Japanese version of the traditional classic European chef's knife shape. Or, if you have chef-like aspirations, purchase a 10-in [25-cm] classic chef's knife. Once you get used to it, the extended length makes chopping less work and more fun. Whichever knife you choose, always rinse and dry the knife by hand and never put it in the dishwasher, as the heat tends to dull the blade.

Keep your knives sharp. When you buy the knife, invest in a steel as well. The steel actually keeps your knife sharp so that it doesn't have to be professionally sharpened quite as often. Ask the salesperson to demonstrate how to steel the knife or check out the technique online. Knives do require professional sharpening once a year or so. I take mine to our local farmers' market where a knife sharpener has a stall, but your local butcher may sharpen your knives for a fee if you ask them nicely.

Use a large cutting board. A 20-in [50-cm] or larger cutting board will give you plenty of room to cut all your fresh vegetables, and if it's plastic or composite it can be washed in the dishwasher as well. Make sure to dry it thoroughly before you stow it away as it can mildew if stacked damp.

Pay attention to how you cut your veggies. The recipes in this book direct you to cut the vegetables a certain way so the ingredients will cook evenly and quickly (and the finished dish will look lovely as well). Make the cuts according to the recipe and your dinner will be on the table in no time flat.

Buy a box of kosher salt. Keep salt in a little bowl beside the stove so that you can grab it with your fingers and add it to food. The clean flavor of kosher salt is vastly superior to regular iodized salt, which can add a metallic taste to dishes. And don't be shy with it. You are cooking fresh food, and for the best flavor, it needs to be seasoned.

Use freshly ground black pepper. The flavor is more robust than packaged ground pepper. To give your food more oomph, buy a peppermill (it needn't be expensive), fill it up with whole black peppercorns (I like Tellicherry peppercorns for their spicy heat), and grind them directly onto your food while it's still cooking. Even if you don't like the heat of pepper, a light sprinkling of it will liven up your dishes without making it too hot.

Try new foods! Ethnic ingredients inject food with interesting flavors. Trying new dishes is fun and keeps the dinner table fresh and interesting. The spices and condiments called for in this book, such as garam masala, chipotle, and Thai fish sauce, are used in multiple recipes, so you should be able to use them up over time. Take a cruise down the international aisle at your grocery store or, better yet, seek out ethnic markets where you can buy these staples on the cheap. If you can't find some of the ingredients locally, stock up online.

Extra-virgin olive oil is a healthy option for cooking. The general rule is to use extra-virgin olive oil, which is more expensive, for salads and uncooked foods and regular olive oil and vegetable oil for cooking. I prefer expeller-pressed vegetable oils, which are processed without extra chemicals or heat, making them a healthier option.

Low-sodium vegetable and chicken broths add extra flavor. The best way to buy broths is in aseptic or cardboard containers. Just use what you need, close the spout, and store it in the fridge for up to a week; it will be ready and waiting for the next time you want more depth in a dish.

No need for precise measuring. I don't want you to spend time measuring when it isn't necessary, so my recipes direct you to chop a whole onion or slice a whole carrot instead of measuring a certain amount of chopped onion or sliced carrots. If you buy the

onions that come in a 3-lb [1.4-kg] mesh bag, they will be just the right size. If they're a little small and you like onion a lot, go ahead and use another one as well. And if they are really big, just use a quarter or half and save the leftover in a sealed plastic bag in the refrigerator. Onions should be about 2 1/2 in [6 cm] in diameter. Carrots should be 10 to 12 in [25 to 30.5 cm] long. Zucchini should be about 8 in [20 cm] long and shallots about 3 in [7.5 cm] long.

Fresh garlic is a must. A head of garlic will keep for weeks in a bowl on your counter. Garlic preferences are personal, so if the cloves are small and you like a lot of garlic, add another clove. Likewise, if the cloves are large and the recipe calls for two, one may be enough.

Shallots are like baby red onions. They are mild and sweet and perfect to use raw for flavoring vinaigrettes or to cook up with mushrooms or other lightly sautéed vegetables. Store them with the garlic on your counter.

Pound your chicken. Chicken breasts should be pounded to an even thickness for faster cooking. Purchase a meat pounder and flatten the fatter end of the breast down. That way it will cook more evenly and quickly.

Use good-quality wine in recipes. When using wine in a recipe, always use dry wine and never use cooking wine, as it's salted and unpalatable. If you don't have leftover wine or don't want to use wine, use broth, fruit juice, or water. I have great success using orange and even cranberry juice in place of wine.

Hot sauces aren't just for pepper heads.
Stock up on sambal oelek or chili-garlic sauce, Sriracha, or whatever hot sauce appeals to you. Just a dash will add layers of flavor to your dinner. A few extra dashes will add heat if you like it hot.

Never underestimate the power of the egg.
Eggs are one of the easiest of dinner fallbacks. If you have eggs, you have a potential dinner. If you have some grated cheese, even better.

Peel ginger with a spoon.
There are a few recipes that incorporate spicy fresh ginger into the meal. The simplest way to peel it is with the edge of a spoon. It's super easy and you don't waste as much ginger as you do when peeling it with a knife.

Handle chiles with gloves.
The seeds and ribs are the hottest parts of the chile, so avoid them if you can. And always test the heat by tasting a tiny piece of chile before tossing the whole thing into a recipe. Sometimes they're hot and sometimes they're not.

Make the most of frozen rice and cooked grains to extend meals.
Many supermarkets sell plain grains like brown and white rice, quinoa, farro, and even some blends with vegetables and seasonings in the freezer case in microwavable bags. Just nuke the package according to the directions and it's ready to go.

Serve meals on heated plates.
Heat plates (with no metal decorations) in the microwave for about 1 1/2 minutes prior to serving up dinner. It's amazing how much longer your food will stay hot on the plate, allowing you to linger and discuss the events of the day with your family.

Serve special drinks for the kids.
I've provided you with adult beverage options but don't want to leave the kids out of the fun. I often serve my granddaughters half juice and half sparkling water mocktails when we are celebrating. They love to be in on the party as well and sometimes they come up with great combinations such as cider and ginger ale mojitos and cranberry and orange juice spritzers. I am aware of the sugar in these drinks and advocate serving them on special occasions and watered down with sparkling water. They love the bubbles so much that they hardly notice that the sugar content has been lowered substantially. I also buy organic juices when possible from brands that I trust. You'll find suggestions for these drinks along with the adult pairings in "In the Glass," so the kids can enjoy a special beverage along with their parents. They will love the special attention, and who doesn't want a blue drink with a gummy fish floating in the glass?

Veggie Good

Pizza with Pesto,

GRAPE TOMATOES, and MOZZARELLA

In the quest to make fresh pizza, frozen-refrigerated pizza dough has become my new best friend. My kitchen doesn't get messy making dough and I don't have to wait for it to rise and proof. If only all my friends were so thoughtful. A version of the classic Margherita, this pizza is simply perfect. Pesto is the quintessential taste and smell of summer, so with a slather of pesto, a scatter of grape tomatoes, and a sprinkle of cheese, *voilà*, a fresh and summery pizza can appear on the dinner table twelve months of the year.

---

10 oz [285 g] grape tomatoes

2 garlic cloves

1 lb [455 g] frozen pizza dough, thawed and out of the refrigerator for about 10 minutes

1 Tbsp olive oil

1/3 cup [75 g] pesto, store-bought or homemade

Kosher salt and freshly ground black pepper

1 1/2 cups [120 g] shredded mozzarella cheese

1/4 cup [20 g] grated Parmesan cheese

---

1. If you have a pizza stone, place it on the bottom rack of the oven. If you don't have a stone, you can bake the pizza on a rimless sheet pan. (It won't be as crispy on the bottom and may take a few more minutes to bake.) Preheat the oven to 450°F [230°C].

2. On a large cutting board, halve the tomatoes and mince the garlic.

3. On a lightly floured surface, pat and stretch out the dough into a 16-in [40.5-cm] circle and place it on a sheet of parchment paper. Transfer the dough and parchment to a pizza peel or a sheet pan. Drizzle the dough with the olive oil, rub the garlic over the top with your fingers, and layer on the pesto, tomatoes, a few sprinkles of salt, a few grinds of pepper, the mozzarella, and the Parmesan.

4. Slide the pizza, still on the parchment, onto the heated pizza stone or transfer the sheet pan to the oven. Bake until the bottom is crispy and the cheese has browned slightly, about 15 minutes.

5. Slide the peel under the pizza to remove it from the oven or transfer the sheet pan to a wire rack and let the pizza cool for about 5 minutes before cutting into wedges. Serve hot.

continued

VEGGIE GOOD

It's that easy: Use a mix of red, orange, and yellow tomatoes for the most beautiful pizza ever.

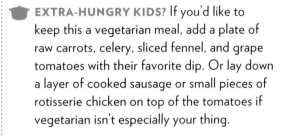

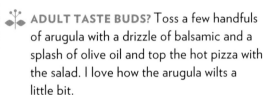

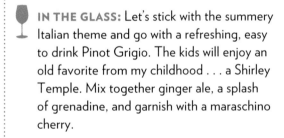

EXTRA-HUNGRY KIDS? If you'd like to keep this a vegetarian meal, add a plate of raw carrots, celery, sliced fennel, and grape tomatoes with their favorite dip. Or lay down a layer of cooked sausage or small pieces of rotisserie chicken on top of the tomatoes if vegetarian isn't especially your thing.

ADULT TASTE BUDS? Toss a few handfuls of arugula with a drizzle of balsamic and a splash of olive oil and top the hot pizza with the salad. I love how the arugula wilts a little bit.

IN THE GLASS: Let's stick with the summery Italian theme and go with a refreshing, easy to drink Pinot Grigio. The kids will enjoy an old favorite from my childhood . . . a Shirley Temple. Mix together ginger ale, a splash of grenadine, and garnish with a maraschino cherry.

Pimiento Grilled Cheese

SANDWICHES

You don't have to hail from below the Mason-Dixon Line to be familiar with pimiento cheese. It's usually spread on crackers for a snack, but this blend of cheese, mayo, and sweet roasted peppers makes the most heavenly grilled cheese sandwiches you've ever tried. I've kept it simple here with sharp Cheddar, but feel free to go rogue and mix it up with equal parts smoked Gouda and mozzarella for a delish change-up.

1 large tomato

8 oz [230 g] sharp Cheddar cheese, grated

One 4-oz [115-g] jar diced pimientos, drained

*¼ cup [60 g] mayonnaise,
plus more for spreading on the bread*

1 Tbsp Dijon mustard

1 Tbsp Worcestershire sauce

2 tsp fresh lemon juice

1 tsp hot sauce, plus more if needed

Kosher salt and freshly ground black pepper

8 slices country-style multigrain bread

Sliced dill pickle spears (optional)

1. On a large cutting board, thinly slice the tomato.

2. In a medium bowl, combine the cheese, pimientos, mayonnaise, mustard, Worcestershire, lemon juice, and hot sauce. Season with salt, pepper, and additional hot sauce to taste.

3. Thinly spread one side of each slice of bread with mayonnaise. Flip four of the slices over to the non-mayo side and top with the cheese mixture and slices of tomato. Top with the remaining bread slices, mayo side out.

4. Heat a 12-in [30.5-cm] skillet over medium heat. Add two of the sandwiches to the pan and cook, pushing down on them to compress, until browned, about 3 minutes. Flip them over and brown the other side, another 3 minutes. (If the sandwiches are browning too fast, reduce the heat to medium-low.) Transfer the sandwiches to a plate and keep warm while repeating the process with the remaining sandwiches.

5. Cut the sandwiches in half and serve with pickles, if desired.

continued

VEGGIE GOOD

It's that easy: Spread your bread with mayo instead of butter. It browns beautifully and, as Forrest Gump says, "It's one less thing."

EXTRA-HUNGRY KIDS? Open a can of tomato soup and warm it up in the same skillet you used for the sandwiches. Or add a few slices of cooked bacon or deli ham to the sandwiches before cooking.

ADULT TASTE BUDS? Add pickled jalapeños to the adult sandwiches.

IN THE GLASS: It totally depends on what you're in the mood for. If using the jalapeños on the sandwich, look for an off-dry Riesling. If you leave the peppers off, a Zinfandel would be the perfect partner. Serve the kids a Blue Ocean, a drink made with watered-down blue punch or Gatorade and a red Swedish fish dropped in to swim.

Potato Casserole

with SWISS CHARD

If hot, cheesy potatoes take you to your happy place, this recipe welcomes you home. Red-skinned potatoes roasted with shallot, garlic, and rosemary are topped with an eggy custard, transforming this side dish into a main meal on those nights when you choose to go meatless. Conversely, this casserole makes a great side to a rotisserie chicken or grilled pork tenderloin.

2 lb [910 g] red potatoes	*1 bunch Swiss chard*
1 shallot	*3 eggs*
2 garlic cloves	*1½ cups [360 ml] half-and-half*
1 Tbsp olive oil	*2 tsp Dijon mustard*
1 sprig rosemary	*1 cup [80 g] grated Gruyère or Swiss cheese*
Kosher salt and freshly ground black pepper	*¼ cup [20 g] grated Parmesan cheese*

1. Preheat the oven to 425°F [220°C].

2. On a large cutting board, halve and thinly slice the potatoes (do not peel) and chop the shallot and garlic.

3. Heat a 12-in [30.5-cm] ovenproof skillet over medium-high heat and add the olive oil. When the oil shimmers, add the potatoes, shallot, garlic, and rosemary along with 1 tsp salt and a few grinds of pepper. Toss to combine and cook, stirring every now and then, for 5 minutes to get things really hot. Transfer the skillet to the oven and roast the potatoes until almost tender, about 15 minutes.

4. While the potatoes roast, remove the ribs from the chard leaves; chop the ribs and leaves and set aside in separate piles.

5. In a medium bowl, whisk the eggs, half-and-half, and mustard along with ½ tsp salt and a few grinds of pepper to make a custard.

6. Return the skillet to the stovetop over medium-high heat (careful; the handle is hot) and add the chard ribs; cook, stirring every now and then, until almost tender, about 2 minutes. Add the leaves to the pan in bunches, adding more as each previous bunch wilts, and cook until tender, about 2 minutes. Check the potatoes with the tip of a knife to make sure they're soft. If they aren't, cook another couple of minutes and check again. The potatoes must be tender before adding the custard. Discard the rosemary sprig and taste, adding more salt or pepper if it needs it.

7. Reduce the oven temperature to 350°F [180°C].

8. Rearrange the potatoes in the skillet to an even thickness. Pour the custard over the potatoes, sprinkle the cheeses over the top, and return the skillet to the oven. Bake the gratin until the custard is set, about 10 minutes.

9. Divide the gratin among heated plates and serve hot.

It's that easy: I like to leave the skins on my potatoes, which will save you prep time, and you don't chop the rosemary either, but if you're having a tough day and you'd like to make this recipe even easier to accomplish, simply add 5 oz [140 g] of baby spinach to the potatoes instead of the Swiss chard. No chopping or trimming required.

 EXTRA-HUNGRY KIDS? Butter toasted rye bread and serve the potatoes on top.

 ADULT TASTE BUDS? Serve with a side of halved grape tomatoes, torn fresh basil, a splash of balsamic vinegar, and a glug of olive oil.

 IN THE GLASS: Pinot Noir is probably the most food-friendly red wine. Look for a bottle from A to Z Winery for a good weeknight value. For the kiddies, serve half lemonade and half sparkling water with a fun straw.

Sweet Potato Gratin

with SPINACH

It can be tough to come up with filling and nutritious vegetarian options for families, but this recipe really comes to the dinner rescue. Good-for-you sweet potatoes, loaded with carotene, plus iron-rich spinach are held together with a tasty cinnamon-flavored custard. Kids of all ages love this dish and I'm guessing it will find its way to dinner plates as a side dish as well.

2 lb [910 g] sweet potatoes	*1 cup [240 ml] half-and-half*
1 shallot	*1 cup [240 g] ricotta cheese*
1 Tbsp olive oil	*¹/₂ tsp ground cinnamon*
Kosher salt and freshly ground black pepper	*10 oz [280 g] baby spinach*
3 eggs	

1. Preheat the oven to 425°F [220°C].

2. On a large cutting board, peel, quarter, and thinly slice the potatoes and chop the shallot.

3. Heat a 12-in [30.5-cm] ovenproof skillet over medium-high heat and add the olive oil. When the oil shimmers, add the potatoes and shallot along with 1 tsp salt and a few grinds of pepper. Toss to combine and cook, stirring every now and then, for 5 minutes or until the potatoes begin to soften. Transfer the pan to the oven and roast the potatoes for 15 minutes or until tender.

4. In a medium bowl, beat together the eggs, half-and-half, ricotta, and cinnamon along with ¹/₂ tsp salt and a few grinds of pepper to make a custard.

5. Return the potatoes to the stovetop over medium-high heat (careful; the handle is hot) and add the spinach in bunches, stirring and adding more as each previous bunch wilts. Check the potatoes with the tip of a knife to make sure they're soft. If they aren't, cook another couple of minutes and check again. The potatoes must be fully cooked before adding the custard. Taste, adding more salt or pepper if it needs it.

6. Reduce the oven temperature to 350°F [180°C].

7. Pour the custard into the hot pan and return it to the oven. Bake until the custard is set, about 10 minutes.

8. Divide the gratin among heated plates and serve hot.

It's that easy: *Slicing the potatoes as thinly as you can helps them cook faster, getting dinner on the table sooner.*

 **EXTRA-HUNGRY KIDS?** Toast slices of raisin bread, butter them, and serve the gratin on top.

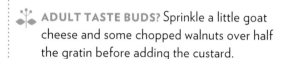 **ADULT TASTE BUDS?** Sprinkle a little goat cheese and some chopped walnuts over half the gratin before adding the custard.

 **IN THE GLASS:** Look for a wine with sweet notes, like an off-dry Riesling, to go with this sweet potato gratin. A bottle of Fern-grove Riesling Off-Dry Limited Release (Australia) partnered with this gratin will get rave reviews.

START TO FINISH
30 minutes
...
HANDS-ON TIME
25 minutes
...
SERVES
4-6

Cheesy Angel Hair Pasta

with ASPARAGUS and BASIL

Angel hair pasta is just so poetic: delicate yet chewy and with a simple cheesy sauce *plus* melted fresh mozzarella on top. Perfect in early spring with slender stalks of asparagus, shiitake mushrooms, and fresh basil, this quick and simple meal checks all the boxes. I hope you like this dish as much as I do.

1 onion

8 oz [230 g] shiitake or cremini mushrooms, tough stems discarded

2 garlic cloves

1 lb [455 g] asparagus, woody ends trimmed

2 cups [12 g] loosely packed fresh basil

1 Tbsp olive oil

Kosher salt and freshly ground black pepper

2 cups [425 ml] vegetable broth

One 15-oz [425-g] can diced tomatoes with juice

One 9-oz [255-g] package fresh angel hair pasta

4 oz [115 g] fresh mozzarella cheese

1 cup [240 g] ricotta cheese

1. On a large cutting board, chop the onion, slice the mushrooms, and mince the garlic. Transfer it all to a medium bowl. Cut the asparagus into 1-in [2.5-cm] pieces and chop the basil. Set aside in separate piles.

2. Heat a 12-in [30.5-cm] ovenproof skillet over medium-high heat and add the olive oil. When the oil shimmers, add the onion mixture to the pan along with ½ tsp salt and a few grinds of pepper. Cook, stirring, until the onion and mushrooms soften, about 3 minutes.

3. Add the broth, tomatoes, angel hair, asparagus, and ½ tsp salt, pushing down so that the pasta and

vegetables are immersed in the liquid. Cover and simmer for 5 minutes.

4. While the pasta simmers, cut the mozzarella into thin slices.

5. Preheat the broiler with the rack in the second-highest position.

6. Stir the ricotta into the skillet with the pasta mixture and taste, adding more salt or pepper if it needs it. Top with the mozzarella and transfer the pan to the oven. Broil until the cheese melts, about 2 minutes.

continued

7. Divide the pasta among heated plates and sprinkle with the chopped basil. Serve hot.

It's that easy: *I've never enjoyed the two-step process of making pasta for dinner. For some reason, I really don't like to cook pasta and then cook the sauce and then toss it all together, so I love this method of cooking the pasta in the pan with the sauce. It's amazing how well it works with the starch from the pasta thickening the sauce. It's what I call a win-win.*

EXTRA-HUNGRY KIDS? Toss $1/2$ cup [60 g] of frozen edamame in with the vegetables for a little added protein.

ADULT TASTE BUDS? It's so simple, but a sprinkle of red pepper flakes really takes this plate to the next level.

IN THE GLASS: A bubbly Prosecco is perfect with this springy dish and even better if eaten outside on a warm spring evening. For the kids, sparkling cider.

START TO FINISH
30 minutes
...
HANDS-ON TIME
30 minutes
...
SERVES
6

SPRING MUSHROOM *and*

Pea Risotto

Risotto is thought by many to be labor-intensive and not for the rookie chef to attempt. Nothing could be further from the truth! Risotto is actually a very simple dish using simple ingredients that come together in a meal that is truly elegant. The main thing is to use a good broth (organic vegetable broth) and the right rice (Arborio or Carnaroli), and to season it with good Parmigiano-Reggiano cheese. To make it even more like dinner, I've added bright peas and meaty mushrooms—classic flavors to include in risotto.

3 cups [720 ml] vegetable broth

1 onion

8 oz [230 g] shiitake mushrooms, tough stems discarded

4 Tbsp [55 g] unsalted butter

1 ³/₄ cups [350 g] Arborio or Carnaroli rice

Kosher salt and freshly ground black pepper

¹/₂ cup [120 ml] white wine

1 cup [120 g] peas, thawed if frozen

¹/₃ cup [80 ml] half-and-half

¹/₂ cup [40 g] freshly grated Parmigiano-Reggiano, plus more for sprinkling

2 Tbsp minced fresh chives

2 tsp fresh lemon juice

1. Heat the broth and 1 cup [240 ml] water in a large measuring cup in the microwave until hot.

2. On a large cutting board, finely dice the onion and slice the mushrooms.

3. In a 4-qt [3.8-L] saucepan, melt 2 Tbsp of the butter over medium heat. Add the onion and mushrooms and cook until softened, about 3 minutes. Add the rice, ¹/₂ tsp salt, and a few grinds of pepper and stir to coat with the butter. Cook, stirring, until the rice is opaque or cloudy-looking, 3 to 4 minutes.

4. Add the wine to the pan, and cook, stirring, until all the wine has been absorbed, about 1 minute. Pour about 1 cup [240 ml] of the warm broth into the pan and cook, stirring, until it is mostly absorbed, about 3 minutes. Add another 1 cup [240 ml] of the broth and stir. Reduce the heat so that the rice is slowly bubbling and stir every now and then, adding more broth when the risotto is no longer soupy. Continue to add broth when the liquid is absorbed and stir every now and then, until the rice is tender and

continued

creamy and still a little al dente, about 15 to 20 minutes. Stir in the remaining 2 Tbsp butter, the peas, half-and-half, cheese, chives, and lemon juice and cook for 1 minute. Taste and season with salt and pepper if it needs it. Stir in more broth or water if you like your risotto extra saucy.

5. Serve immediately in heated bowls with a sprinkle of Parmigiano-Reggiano on top.

It's that easy: Contrary to popular culinary wisdom, it's not necessary to stir risotto constantly. The important phase is in the beginning when you stir the first batch of broth into the rice. After that an occasional stir is all the rice needs. But finished risotto waits for no man. Take little bites every few minutes after it has cooked for 15 minutes to check the rice's progress (no chalky texture, look for just al dente) because when the risotto is perfectly cooked, it's best to eat it right away.

EXTRA-HUNGRY KIDS? If you don't need this dish to be vegetarian, a cup of diced ham added at the end with the peas is a nice way to boost the heartiness.

ADULT TASTE BUDS? If you have truffle oil, a drizzle of it is sublime.

IN THE GLASS: What else but a chilled bottle of Sauvignon Blanc? For a splurge, try Cloudy Bay, a favorite of mine.

Asian Brussels Sprouts

with BROWN RICE

Did you know that Brussels sprouts are high in protein, vitamin A, folate, potassium, and calcium? These tiny cabbages are not only cute, but they are also extremely delicious when roasted in a hot, hot oven. The browned and nutty nuggets are then tossed with an Asian vinaigrette, raisins, hazelnuts, mint, and cilantro and served over good-for-you brown rice for a meal that really satisfies.

---

1 lb [455 g] Brussels sprouts

1 shallot

1 garlic clove

1 Tbsp vegetable oil

Kosher salt and freshly ground black pepper

¼ cup [35 g] raisins

Two 8- to 10-oz [227- to 283-g] bags frozen precooked brown rice

1 Tbsp sugar

1 Tbsp rice vinegar

1 Tbsp lime juice

1½ tsp soy sauce

1 tsp Asian sesame oil

¼ cup [30 g] chopped hazelnuts

¼ cup [10 g] chopped fresh cilantro

2 Tbsp chopped fresh mint

---

1. Line a sheet pan with aluminum foil and place it in the oven. Preheat the oven to 425°F [220°C].

2. On a large cutting board, quarter the Brussels sprouts and chop the shallot and garlic. Transfer the vegetables to a medium bowl and toss with the vegetable oil and a sprinkle of salt and a few grinds of pepper.

3. Remove the sheet pan from the oven and spread the sprout mixture evenly on the hot pan. Roast until the sprouts are tender and browned around the edges, about 15 minutes.

4. Meanwhile, place the raisins in a small bowl and cover with hot tap water. Cook the rice according to the package directions.

5. In a large bowl, combine 1 Tbsp water with the sugar, vinegar, lime juice, soy sauce, and sesame oil and stir to dissolve the sugar.

6. Drain the raisins and add them to the vinegar mixture along with the hazelnuts, cilantro, and mint. Add the cooked sprouts, toss to coat well, and add more salt and pepper if it needs it.

7. Divide the rice among heated bowls and top each with the veggie mixture. Pour any remaining liquid from the bowl over the vegetables. Serve hot.

It's that easy: Don't shy away from buying these Asian ingredients; you will undoubtedly use them up when cooking other recipes from this book. I love rice vinegar for its tart yet sweet edge, and just a touch of Asian sesame oil injects loads of flavor to dishes. Be sure to keep the sesame oil in the fridge after opening, as it can go rancid quickly.

EXTRA-HUNGRY KIDS? Add a drained can of baby corn to the Brussels sprouts during the last 5 minutes of cooking time. Kids just love those tiny ears.

ADULT TASTE BUDS? Add a few Tbsp of chopped spicy kimchi. It's delish.

IN THE GLASS: Look for a white wine with high acid and a little residual sweetness like a Chenin Blanc, Vouvray, or dry Riesling. For the kids, start with a fun glass and add sparkling water, a splash of maraschino cherry juice, and a cherry.

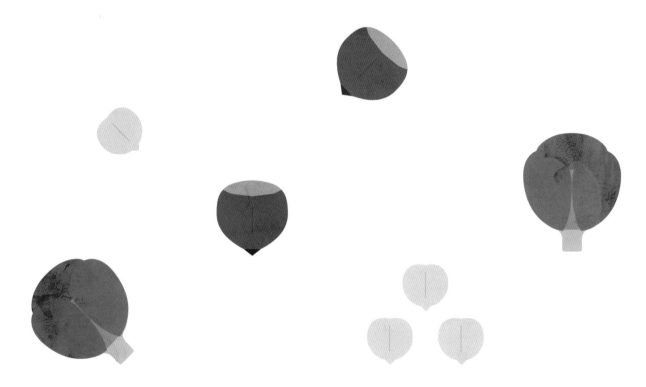

Roasted Broccoli

with PEANUTS and BROWN RICE

When my kids were growing up, they didn't always like vegetables, but I could always get them to eat broccoli as long as it had a sauce. I sometimes joke that even an old shoe would be delicious with this Thai-inspired peanut sauce, and that might be true, but my kids thought this lightly spicy peanut-y sauce made simple roasted broccoli into an actual treat.

2 bunches broccoli	¼ cup [40 ml] plus 2 tsp rice vinegar or cider vinegar
1 red onion	¼ cup [50 g] packed brown sugar
2 garlic cloves	2 tsp Asian sesame oil
1 Tbsp vegetable oil	1 tsp chili-garlic sauce or pinch of red pepper flakes
Kosher salt and freshly ground black pepper	Two 8- to 10-oz [227- to 283-g] bags frozen precooked rice
⅓ cup [70 g] smooth or chunky peanut butter	
2 Tbsp soy sauce	⅓ cup [45 g] chopped peanuts

1. Line a sheet pan with aluminum foil and place it in the oven. Preheat the oven to 425°F [220°C].

2. On a large cutting board, cut the broccoli lengthwise into ¼- to ½-in [6- to 12-mm] slices and transfer it to a large bowl. Slice the onion, chop the garlic, and combine them with the broccoli, vegetable oil, ½ tsp salt, and a few grinds of pepper.

3. Remove the sheet pan from the oven and spread the vegetables evenly on the hot pan. Roast until the broccoli is tender, about 20 minutes.

4. While the vegetables cook, stir together the peanut butter, soy sauce, vinegar, sugar, sesame oil, and chili-garlic sauce in a medium bowl.

5. Steam the rice according to the package directions and divide it among heated bowls. Top the rice with the roasted broccoli mixture and drizzle with the peanut sauce. Sprinkle with the peanuts and serve.

It's that easy: The peanut sauce is wonderful tossed with noodles or used as a dipping sauce with rotisserie chicken, so make up a double batch to keep on hand. You can store it in the fridge for a week, but it will be gone long before then.

 **EXTRA-HUNGRY KIDS?** Warm some drained canned chickpeas in the microwave and stir them into the rice.

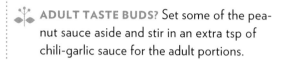 **ADULT TASTE BUDS?** Set some of the peanut sauce aside and stir in an extra tsp of chili-garlic sauce for the adult portions.

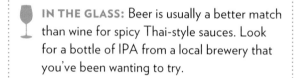 **IN THE GLASS:** Beer is usually a better match than wine for spicy Thai-style sauces. Look for a bottle of IPA from a local brewery that you've been wanting to try.

START TO FINISH
40 minutes
...
HANDS-ON TIME
30 minutes
...
SERVES
4

PARMESAN-CRUSTED

Cauliflower Steaks

with FARRO

Cauliflower has become the Pygmalion vegetable of the century since we found out that roasting the heck out of it reveals its delicious sweetness—it's become the star of the dinner show. Roasting removes some of the water in the vegetable, which concentrates the sugars, and then there's the browning of those sugars in a hot, hot oven, making this vegetable the opposite of what you might have grown up eating. I've topped these "steaks" with a mix of bread crumbs and Parmesan for crunch and a touch of saltiness. Your favorite marinara gives it a flash of color. Meatless dinner never tasted so good.

1 large head cauliflower	*¼ cup [20 g] grated Parmesan cheese*
3 Tbsp olive oil	*¼ cup [15 g] panko bread crumbs*
Kosher salt and freshly ground black pepper	*Two 8- to 10-oz [227- to 283-g] bags frozen precooked farro*
¼ cup [35 g] raisins	*2 cups [460 g] jarred marinara sauce*
1 egg	

1. Line a sheet pan with aluminum foil and place it in the oven. Preheat the oven to 425°F [220°C].

2. Trim the stem and leaves from the bottom of the cauliflower and cut the head in half through the center of the stem. Cut each half in the same direction into slices that are ³⁄₄ to 1 in [2 to 2.5 cm] thick. Some of the florets will fall off, but you should have about six steaks and lots of florets. Cook them all. You'll be glad you did.

3. Remove the sheet pan from the oven and arrange the cauliflower steaks and any extra florets in a single layer on the hot pan. Brush the cauliflower steaks and florets with 2 Tbsp of the olive oil, and sprinkle with ¹⁄₂ tsp salt and a few grinds of pepper. Roast until it begins to soften, about 20 minutes.

4. Meanwhile, place the raisins in small dish with hot tap water to cover and set aside to plump. Beat the egg in a small dish along with a sprinkle of salt and a few grinds of pepper. In a small bowl, combine the Parmesan and panko with the remaining 1 Tbsp olive oil with a fork.

5. Remove the pan from the oven, brush the cauliflower with the beaten egg, and sprinkle the panko mixture generously over the tops. Return the pan to the oven and cook until the cauliflower is tender and the topping has browned, about 10 minutes. (You can broil the cauliflower on the second-highest rack for about 30 seconds or so if the cheese isn't browned enough, but watch it closely or it will burn.)

6. While the cauliflower is cooking, cook the farro according to the package directions and heat the marinara in the microwave. Drain the raisins and toss them with the farro, a few sprinkles of salt, and a few grinds of pepper.

7. Divide the farro among heated plates, top with cauliflower and spoonfuls of marinara, and serve hot.

It's that easy: Heads of cauliflower can differ in size, so if the heads are small you may need two heads to feed four. It's never a bad thing to have leftover roasted cauliflower. It tastes great the next day.

EXTRA-HUNGRY KIDS? In a pinch, I like to serve Progresso soup, and the minestrone would be perfect with the marinara-topped cauliflower.

ADULT TASTE BUDS? Add a few chopped Kalamata olives and a tsp of sweet pickle relish to the cheesy panko mixture after topping the kid's vegetables. Salty plus sweet and sour equals delish.

IN THE GLASS: A Spanish Albariño is a terrific bottle to drink with this light meal; it's crisp, with notes of apple and melon. Look for a bottle by La Caña. The kids might like a glass of half white grape juice and half sparkling water, garnished with an orange slice.

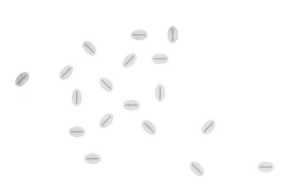

ROOT VEGETABLE

Quinoa Bowl

with TAHINI

You'll see lots of root vegetables in this book because (1) I love their sweet taste, especially when roasted; (2) they keep in the fridge for weeks, waiting patiently to be cooked up; and (3) they're filling and delicious year-round when the more tender local summer vegetables are nowhere to be found. The simplicity of this meal is staggering, and because the vegetables are paired with creamy tahini sauce, chickpeas, and quinoa for protein, even my husband doesn't miss the meat.

2 large bulbs fennel, about 1 lb [455 g]

2 medium sweet potatoes, about 12 oz [340 g]

2 large carrots, about 6 oz [170 g]

2 large parsnips, about 6 oz [170 g]

10 radishes

2 Tbsp olive oil

Kosher salt and freshly ground black pepper

Two 8- to 10-oz [227- to 283-g] bags frozen precooked quinoa

One 15-oz [430-g] can chickpeas, drained and rinsed

1/3 cup [40 g] pine nuts (optional)

Tahini Sauce

1 garlic clove

1/3 cup [75 g] tahini

Juice of 1 lemon

Pinch of red pepper flakes

Kosher salt and freshly ground black pepper

1/4 cup [10 g] chopped fresh flat-leaf parsley

1. Line a sheet pan with aluminum foil and place it in the oven. Preheat the oven to 450°F [230°C].

2. On a large cutting board, quarter and core the fennel and cut it into 1-in [2.5-cm] slices; transfer to a large bowl. Peel and quarter the sweet potatoes, cut them into 1/2-in [12-mm] pieces, and add to the bowl. Peel and slice the carrots and parsnips into 1/4-in [6-mm] slices and halve the radishes; add them to the bowl. Toss the vegetables with the olive oil, 1 tsp salt, and a few grinds of pepper. Remove the sheet pan from the oven and arrange the vegetables in a single layer on the hot pan. Roast until tender and lightly browned, 20 to 25 minutes. Taste

continued

VEGGIE GOOD

41

and sprinkle with more salt and pepper if it needs it.

3. For the tahini sauce: While the vegetables roast, mince the garlic and transfer to a medium bowl. Add the tahini, lemon juice, red pepper flakes, a pinch of salt, and a few grinds of pepper and stir together with a fork. Stir in 1/3 cup [80 ml] water a few Tbsp at a time (it will thicken before it begins to thin) until it is the texture of yogurt. It may take more or less water. Stir in half the parsley. Set aside.

4. Cook the quinoa according to the package directions.

5. Sprinkle the chickpeas over the vegetables in the pan and roast for another 2 minutes.

6. Divide the quinoa among heated bowls and top with the vegetables. Drizzle each bowl with the tahini sauce and a sprinkle of the remaining parsley and pine nuts, if using. Serve hot.

It's that easy: *Tahini is kind of like the peanut butter of the Middle East. It's made from ground sesame seeds and you can find it in the international aisle at your grocery store. It's one of the main ingredients in hummus, so once you have it on hand you are only a can of chickpeas and a lemon away from making your very own hummus dip.*

EXTRA-HUNGRY KIDS? Wrap the quinoa and tahini-sauced vegetables in flatbread and serve as a wrap.

ADULT TASTE BUDS? Pickled vegetables always wake up my taste buds. Look for a jar of pickled turnips in the international aisle at your grocery. They're a fabulous addition to vegetarian dishes or Middle Eastern–inspired wraps and sandwiches. In a pinch, a chopped dill pickle will do.

IN THE GLASS: An easy-to-drink Pinot Grigio is terrific. Santa Margherita is one of my favorites, but the lower-priced Kris Pinot Grigio would be a good choice as well.

ROASTED VEGETABLE, FETA, *and*

Smoked Almond Salad

We frequently eat salad for dinner at our house, especially in the summer months when high temperatures make lighter and fresher dinners so appealing. But don't think for a moment that our appetites are discouraged by the humid dog days of a Cleveland, Ohio, summer. No wimpy little salad for us. We want to feel like we ate dinner (not to be confused with lunch) even if it is 90 degrees outside, and this salad, packed with tasty roasted vegetables, nuts, and cheese, really satisfies.

2 carrots	*Kosher salt and freshly ground black pepper*
1 red onion	1 small shallot
2 zucchini	1/2 cup [40 g] chopped smoked almonds
2 red bell peppers	2 Tbsp balsamic vinegar
1 lemon	6 large handfuls mixed salad greens, such as Bibb, radicchio, romaine, and arugula
2 garlic cloves	
2 Tbsp plus 1/4 cup [60 ml] extra-virgin olive oil	1/2 cup [60 g] crumbled feta cheese
	1 tsp minced fresh thyme or chives

1. Line a sheet pan with aluminum foil and place it in the oven. Preheat the oven to 425°F [220°C].

2. On a large cutting board, peel the carrots and cut into 1/2-in [12-mm] pieces. Cut the onion into 1/2-in [12-mm] slices, the zucchini into 2-in [5-cm] pieces, and the bell peppers into 2-in [5-cm] squares. As you work, transfer the vegetables to a large bowl. Zest the lemon, chop the garlic, and add them to the bowl, then add 2 Tbsp of the olive oil, 1/2 tsp salt, and a few grinds of pepper and toss to coat.

3. Remove the sheet pan from the oven and arrange the vegetables in a single layer on the hot pan. Roast until tender and lightly browned, 20 to 25 minutes.

4. While the vegetables cook, mince the shallot and squeeze the lemon juice into a small bowl.

continued

5. Sprinkle the almonds over the vegetables during the last 5 minutes of cooking to toast them lightly. Remove the pan from the oven and let cool slightly.

6. In a very large bowl, combine the vinegar with 1 Tbsp lemon juice. Add 2 pinches of salt and the shallot and whisk to combine. Whisk in the remaining 1/4 cup [60 ml] olive oil and taste for seasoning, adding more vinegar, oil, salt, or pepper if it needs it. Add the salad greens to the bowl with the dressing and toss to mix.

7. Divide the dressed greens among plates and top with the warm vegetables, feta cheese, and fresh herbs. Grind a little black pepper over the top and dig in.

It's that easy: *I make it a point to wash greens as soon as I get them home, spin them dry, roll them up in kitchen towels, zip them up in plastic bags, and store them in the crisper drawer of the refrigerator. That way they are always crisp and cold when I need them, instead of watery and limp from a recent wash. I occasionally take advantage of the organic packaged arugula sold in the plastic bin, but I never buy the prewashed, bagged greens anymore because they taste of chemicals and are generally of very poor quality.*

EXTRA-HUNGRY KIDS? Warm a loaf of ciabatta bread in the oven with the vegetables and serve with a plate of olive oil at the table for dipping.

ADULT TASTE BUDS? Instead of feta cheese, add Gorgonzola or Maytag blue cheese to the adult portions.

IN THE GLASS: Grüner, Grüner, Grüner . . . hard to say but so easy to drink, Grüner Veltliner from Austria is a wine you really should get to know. Similar to Chardonnay with hints of pepper and spice, Grüner is a delicious summer quaffer that could become your new warm weather favorite. Serve the kids iced tea with a splash of orange juice and a silly straw.

Roasted Beet Salad

with ORANGES, GOAT CHEESE, and WALNUTS

I didn't always like beets. As a child, the only beet I ever met was canned, and so the avoidance was universally understandable. But I've become a bona fide beet-nik as an adult; a bunch of fresh beets drizzled with olive oil, salt, and pepper and roasted in a hot oven with a clove or two of garlic is a wonderful taste sensation. This salad uses beets at their best.

1 1/2 lb [680 g] beets, trimmed and scrubbed

3 garlic cloves

2 Tbsp plus 1/3 cup [80 ml] olive oil

Kosher salt and freshly ground black pepper

1/2 cup [60 g] chopped walnuts

2 navel oranges

2 Tbsp sherry vinegar

2 tsp grainy Dijon mustard

6 handfuls baby arugula or a mix of arugula and spring greens

1 cup [140 g] crumbled goat cheese

1 baguette

Unsalted butter

1. Place a sheet pan in the oven and preheat the oven to 425°F [220°C].

2. On a large cutting board, cut the beets into bite-size pieces and chop two of the garlic cloves. Divide the beets between two large sheets of aluminum foil, scatter the garlic over the top, drizzle with 2 Tbsp of the olive oil, and sprinkle with 1/2 tsp salt and a few grinds of black pepper. Keeping the beets in a single layer, seal each piece of foil into a packet. Remove the sheet pan from the oven and place both packets on the hot pan. Roast until a sharp knife inserted into the largest chunk offers no resistance, about 30 minutes. Unwrap the beets and let them cool.

3. While the beets cook, place the walnuts on a sheet of foil. Roll up the edges to make a "pan" for them and roast them in the oven with the beets until lightly browned and fragrant, about 5 minutes. Set aside to cool.

4. Grate the zest from one of the oranges into a large bowl. Peel and thinly slice both oranges and transfer them to a small bowl; set aside. Cut the remaining garlic clove in half and add it to the orange zest along with the vinegar and 1/4 tsp salt. Let sit for at least 5 minutes so that the garlic has a chance to flavor the liquid. Scoop out the garlic and discard. Whisk in the mustard, then the remaining

1/3 cup [80 ml] olive oil in a steady stream. Taste the vinaigrette and add more salt and pepper if it needs it. Toss in the warm beets and their juices and coat them with the dressing.

5. Mound the arugula on a serving platter and lay the orange slices on top. Spoon the dressed beets on top of everything and drizzle the salad with the remaining dressing. Sprinkle the goat cheese and walnuts over the top. Serve at the table with the baguette and butter to oohs and aahs.

It's that easy: *Try making this dish with colorful Chioggia beets. When sliced they have charming pink and white rings like a candy cane. I also sometimes combine red and orange beets because they are so beautiful together, but be sure to cook them in separate foil packages because the red beets do not behave and will bleed all over the orange ones.*

EXTRA-HUNGRY KIDS? Spread a layer of hummus on the platter and layer the salad on top. Use pieces of bread to scoop up the hummus after the salad has been served. Fun!

ADULT TASTE BUDS? Top adult portions with an ounce or two of Gorgonzola instead of goat cheese.

IN THE GLASS: A Pinot Noir with a little acid will stand up to the mustard in the vinaigrette. Look out for Elouan Pinot Noir Oregon for a bottle with firm acidity with notes of ripe cherry, red plum, and sweet cinnamon. Serve the kids a glass of half apple juice and half sparkling water with an apple slice and a gummy worm.

Curry Roasted Carrots and Lentils

with ORANGE-YOGURT SAUCE

I love roasted carrots. I really do. When roasted they become sweeter and have a caramelized flavor that I find absolutely addictive. They're even better when tossed with curry powder and slathered with an orangey yogurt sauce. I could eat this dish on a weekly basis, and once you try it, I bet you'll like to as well. For a real treat, try making this dish with rainbow carrots at least once in your life. I'm not sure if the color makes them taste better, but it might!

1¹/₂ lb [680 g] carrots	*1 navel orange*
2 shallots	*2 Tbsp chopped fresh cilantro*
1 Tbsp olive oil	*1 cup [240 g] plain Greek yogurt*
2 tsp curry powder	*One 15-oz [425-g] can lentils*
Kosher salt and freshly ground black pepper	*Two 8- to 10-oz [227- to 283-g] bags frozen precooked quinoa*

1. Line a sheet pan with aluminum foil and place it in the oven. Preheat the oven to 425°F [220°C].

2. On a large cutting board, peel the carrots and slice them thinly. Chop the shallots and transfer them with the carrots to a large bowl. Add the olive oil, curry powder, ¹/₂ tsp salt, and a few grinds of pepper and toss to combine.

3. Remove the sheet pan from the oven and spread the carrots out on the hot pan. Roast for 15 minutes. Check to see if the carrots are done by inserting the tip of a knife into one. They should still be slightly resistant but tender.

4. Zest and juice the orange and combine with the cilantro in a medium bowl. Add the yogurt, a sprinkle of salt, and a few grinds of pepper and stir to combine. Taste and add more salt and pepper if it needs it.

5. Drain and rinse the lentils, stir them into the carrots, and return the pan to the oven for 5 minutes more.

6. Cook the quinoa according to the package directions. Divide the quinoa, carrots, and lentils among heated plates and top with a dollop of yogurt sauce. Serve hot.

It's that easy: *There are many brands of curry powder and they all vary in spice ratios. The only way to find the best one for you is to try a bunch of different brands, so buy them in small amounts so that you can use them up quickly.*

🍲 **EXTRA-HUNGRY KIDS?** Add another can of lentils.

🌿 **ADULT TASTE BUDS?** Add a pinch or two of cayenne to the yogurt sauce after saucing the kids' portions.

🍷 **IN THE GLASS:** Bubbles make any night a party. Try the brut Prosecco from Mionetto for a fruity bouquet with a hint of apples. Kids like bubbles as well! Serve them a non-alcoholic sparkler.

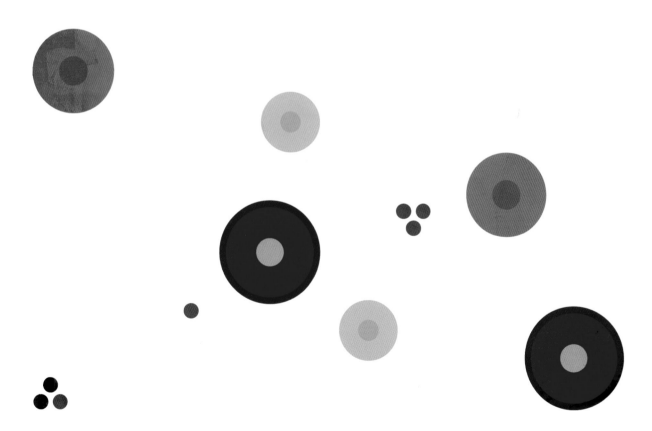

Vegetable Soup

with POACHED EGGS

This weeknight soup is chock-full of fresh vegetables plus a bottle of V-8 juice, so you are really getting your daily dose of vitamins in each steaming bowl. Zucchini, carrots, potato, and sweet potato add color, nutrition, and heft. Move over minestrone, there's a new soup in town.

1 onion	*1 tsp dried oregano*
3 zucchini	*1 tsp kosher salt*
3 carrots	*Freshly ground black pepper*
2 garlic cloves	*4 cups [960 ml] V-8 juice*
1 medium potato	*2 cups [480 ml] vegetable broth*
1 medium sweet potato	*4 eggs*
2 Tbsp olive oil	*2 Tbsp chopped fresh parsley*

1. On a large cutting board, chop the onion; transfer to a medium bowl. Quarter the zucchini lengthwise and slice thinly. Peel and thinly slice the carrots and chop the garlic. Add the zucchini, carrots, and garlic to the bowl with the onion. Peel the potato and sweet potato and cut them into 1/2-in [12-mm] dice; set them aside.

2. Heat a 4-qt [3.8-L] saucepan over medium-high heat and add the olive oil. When the oil shimmers, add the bowl of vegetables, oregano, salt, and a few grinds of pepper and sauté until the vegetables soften somewhat, about 4 minutes. Stir in the potatoes, V-8 juice, and broth and bring to a boil. Reduce the heat to low and simmer until the vegetables are tender and the flavors have blended, about 20 minutes.

3. Carefully break each egg into the soup and cook until they are soft poached, 2 to 3 minutes.

4. Using a large spoon, carefully scoop each cooked egg (so as not to break the yolk) and place in a heated bowl. Ladle the soup over the eggs and sprinkle the bowls with parsley. Serve hot.

It's that easy: *To cut a potato into small dice, first cut it in half lengthwise. Lay it on its flat side and slice it lengthwise into ½-in [12-mm] slices and then lay each of those on their flat sides and cut them again into a french fry shape. Finish by cutting them again crosswise into dice. Once you get the hang of it, you will be able to cut small dice in no time.*

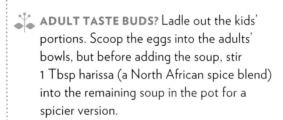 **EXTRA-HUNGRY KIDS?** Add 1 cup [260 g] rinsed canned white beans along with the broth.

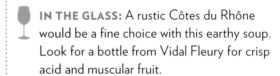 **ADULT TASTE BUDS?** Ladle out the kids' portions. Scoop the eggs into the adults' bowls, but before adding the soup, stir 1 Tbsp harissa (a North African spice blend) into the remaining soup in the pot for a spicier version.

IN THE GLASS: A rustic Côtes du Rhône would be a fine choice with this earthy soup. Look for a bottle from Vidal Fleury for crisp acid and muscular fruit.

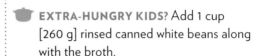

Curried Lentil Soup

Lentils are a standard ingredient in vegetarian homes because they pack a wallop of protein, but they're also filling and tasty to boot. This simple soup is going to charm you with its warm, flavorful Indian spices, creating a more complex flavor profile than these few ingredients would suggest. Drizzled with spiced yogurt sauce, this soup is a real treat.

1 onion	**Spiced Yogurt Sauce**
One 2-in [5-cm] knob fresh ginger	*½ lemon*
2 garlic cloves	*2 Tbsp chopped fresh cilantro*
2 tsp curry powder	*⅓ cup [80 g] plain Greek yogurt*
Pinch of cayenne pepper	*1 Tbsp olive oil*
Pinch of ground cinnamon	*1 tsp honey*
Kosher salt and freshly ground black pepper	*¼ tsp ground cinnamon*
2 Tbsp unsalted butter	*Kosher salt*
6 cups [1.5 L] vegetable broth	*Cayenne pepper*
1¼ cups [250 g] lentils, rinsed and picked through for stones	*Chapati or flour tortillas*

1. On a large cutting board, chop the onion and peel and mince the ginger and garlic. Combine the curry powder, cayenne, cinnamon, ½ tsp salt, and a few grinds of pepper in a small bowl.

2. Heat a 4-qt [3.8 L] saucepan over medium-high heat and add the butter. Add the onion, ginger, garlic, and the spice mixture and sauté, stirring every now and then, until the onion softens, about 3 minutes.

3. Stir in the broth and lentils and bring to a simmer. Reduce the heat to low, cover, and simmer until the lentils are tender, about 20 minutes. Taste, and if the lentils are still a little chewy, give it another 5 minutes.

4. For the spiced yogurt sauce: While the soup cooks, squeeze the lemon into a small bowl and set aside. In a separate small bowl, combine 1 tsp of the lemon juice, 2 tsp of the cilantro, the yogurt, olive oil, honey, cinnamon, a pinch of salt, and a pinch of cayenne. Taste for seasoning and add more salt or cayenne if it needs it. If you'd like to make the yogurt sauce more drizzly, add a Tbsp or more of water to thin it out.

5. With a potato masher, partially smash the lentils in the saucepan to help thicken the soup. Stir in 1 Tbsp of the remaining lemon juice and the remaining cilantro. Taste and add more salt, pepper, cayenne, or lemon juice if it needs it.

6. Ladle the hot soup into heated bowls and drizzle with the yogurt sauce. Serve with the chapati alongside.

It's that easy: *Peeling ginger is easy if you use a spoon. That's right. Just scrape away the outer skin with the tip of a spoon and then slice it and mince with a sharp knife. It's a ginger victory.*

EXTRA-HUNGRY KIDS? Add a few spoonfuls of cooked brown rice at the bottom of the bowl and ladle the soup over the top.

ADULT TASTE BUDS? The yogurt sauce adds oomph. You could also add some halved grape tomatoes that have been tossed with a squeeze of lemon juice, salt, and pepper on top. They add not just color but tasty brightness as well.

IN THE GLASS: A creamy, oaky Chardonnay from Rodney Strong is the perfect sipper with this earthy dinner. Mix up a grape and orange cooler for the kids by combining 2 parts white grape juice with 1 part orange juice and 1 part ginger ale. Garnish with an orange slice.

Sweet Potato Soup

with APPLE-Y CHEESE QUESADILLAS

When I'm looking for a satisfying fall soup, sweet potato is the first to come to mind. Most kids love it, even more so when topped with a little coconut and golden raisins. But don't let that sweet side fool you. This hearty soup is packed with vitamins and good-for-you things that help you run faster, grow taller, and even think smarter. At least that's what I tell my kids.

2½ lb [1.2 kg] sweet potatoes

1 sweet-tart apple, such as Jazz, Crispin, or Braeburn

1 onion

1 garlic clove

⅓ cup [45 g] golden raisins

½ cup [30 g] unsweetened coconut

Four 7-in [18-cm] flour tortillas

6 slices Muenster cheese

4 Tbsp [55 g] unsalted butter

½ tsp dried thyme

Kosher salt and freshly ground black pepper

4 cups [960 ml] vegetable broth

1 cup [240 ml] half-and-half

1. On a large cutting board, peel the sweet potatoes and chop them into 1-in [2.5-cm] pieces; set aside. Peel, core, and thinly slice the apple; chop the onion; and mince the garlic.

2. Put the raisins in a small bowl, cover with hot tap water, and let sit for at least 10 minutes, then drain.

3. Heat a 4-qt [3.8-L] saucepan over medium-high heat and add the coconut. Stir constantly until it turns golden brown, about 3 minutes. Remove the pan from the heat and transfer the coconut to a small bowl to cool.

4. On a work surface, lay out the tortillas and top two of them with the cheese and apple. Top them with the remaining tortillas.

5. Return the pan to medium heat and add 1 Tbsp of the butter. When the butter has melted, add one of the quesadillas, cheese on the bottom (that way the cheese will melt and act like glue, making it easier to flip over) and cook until browned, about 2 minutes. Carefully turn it over with a large spatula to cook the other side, another 2 minutes. Repeat the process, adding another 1 Tbsp butter and the remaining quesadilla. Transfer the quesadillas to a plate, cut in half, and hold in a warm oven.

6. Return the pan to medium-high heat and add the remaining 2 Tbsp butter, onion, garlic, sweet potatoes, thyme, ½ tsp salt, and a few grinds of pepper. Sauté until the onion softens, about 3 minutes. Add the broth and bring to a simmer. Reduce the heat to low and cook at a bare simmer until the potatoes are tender, about 20 minutes.

7. Blend the soup with an immersion blender to make it smooth or just mash up the potatoes with a potato masher for a thicker consistency. Stir in the half-and-half; taste and season the soup with more salt and pepper if it needs it.

8. Ladle the soup into heated bowls and sprinkle with the toasted coconut and plumped raisins. Serve with a half quesadilla on the side.

It's that easy: My grocery store sells sweet potatoes already peeled and chopped. Buying it this way will cost a little more, but will save you time.

 EXTRA-HUNGRY KIDS? Add diced rotisserie chicken to the quesadilla.

 ADULT TASTE BUDS? Ladle up the kids' portions and add 1 tsp curry powder to the remaining soup in the pot. Stir well. You can also add thinly sliced red onion to your quesadilla.

 IN THE GLASS: Your favorite Chardonnay would be perfect.

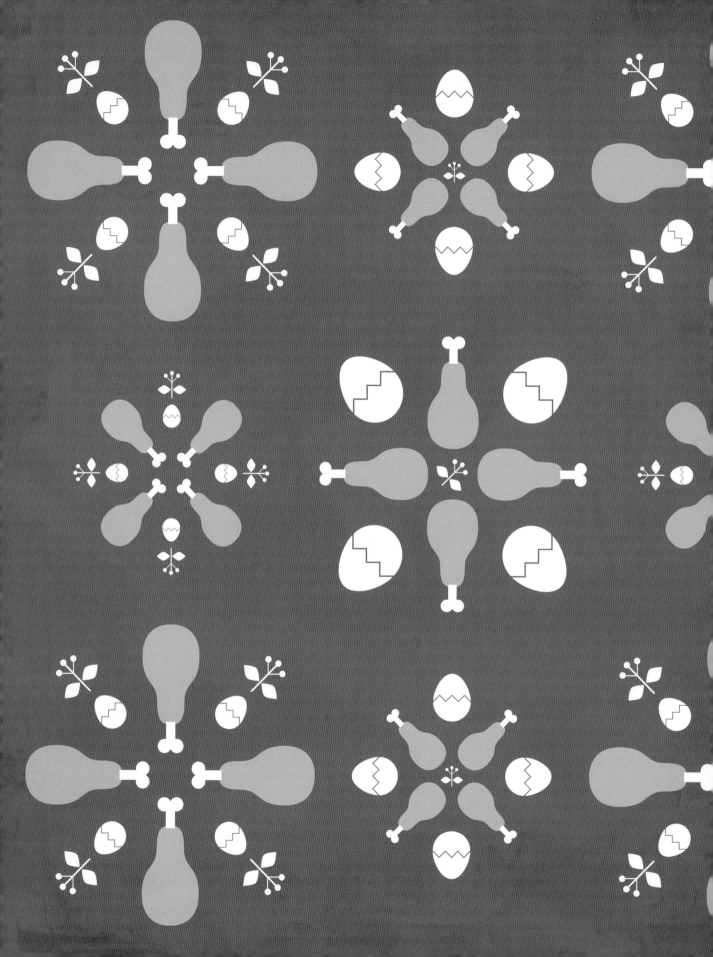

CHAPTER

2

Winner, Winner, Chicken Dinner

White Pizza

with FONTINA, CHICKEN, *and* ARUGULA

I've been making a version of this pizza for the last thirty years and it never fails to please. The garlicky oil base is just right with all that flavorful rotisserie chicken blanketed with Fontina cheese. The arugula salad on top adds a spicy green note to lighten things up and I love how the heat from the pizza wilts the arugula a bit. It's essentially dinner on a pizza.

½ red onion

2 garlic cloves

1 lb [455 g] frozen pizza dough, thawed and out of the refrigerator for about 10 minutes

3 Tbsp olive oil

1½ cups [210 g] shredded rotisserie chicken

Kosher salt and freshly ground black pepper

1½ cups [120 g] grated Fontina cheese

¼ cup [20 g] grated Parmesan cheese

2 tsp white wine vinegar

3 handfuls baby arugula

1. If you have a pizza stone, place it on the bottom rack of the oven. If you don't have a pizza stone, you can bake the pizza on a rimless sheet pan. (It won't be as crispy on the bottom and may take a few more minutes to bake.) Preheat the oven to 450°F [230°C].

2. On a large cutting board, thinly slice the onion and mince the garlic; set aside.

3. On a lightly floured surface, pat and stretch the dough into a 16-in [40.5-cm] circle and place it on a sheet of parchment paper. Transfer the dough and parchment to a pizza peel or a sheet pan. Drizzle the dough with 1½ Tbsp of the olive oil and rub the garlic over the top with your fingers. Layer on

the chicken, sprinkle with salt and a few grinds of pepper, then top it with the Fontina, Parmesan, and red onion.

4. Slide the pizza, still on the parchment, onto the heated pizza stone or transfer the sheet pan to the oven. Bake until the bottom is crispy and the cheese has browned slightly, 12 to 15 minutes.

5. While the pizza cooks, in a large bowl, combine the vinegar, a sprinkle of salt, a few grinds of pepper, and the remaining 1½ Tbsp olive oil and whisk to combine it well. Add the arugula to the bowl and toss with your hands to coat it with the dressing.

continued

6. Slide the peel under the pizza to remove it from the oven or transfer the sheet pan to a wire rack. Arrange the arugula salad on the pizza and let cool for about 5 minutes before cutting into wedges. Serve hot.

It's that easy: Rotisserie chicken comes to the rescue at our house a few times a month. It's great on a pizza but I also use it in quick vegetable-based soups and on simple salads to make dinner more substantial. I have the best results when I shred it as soon as I get it home (it's easier when still warm) and then divvy it up among a few zippered plastic bags. If I don't use it all up within a few days I can toss the remainder in the freezer without even thinking about it.

EXTRA-HUNGRY KIDS? Scatter some rinsed canned white beans on the pizza along with the chicken. They add heft and nutrition and taste great as well.

ADULT TASTE BUDS? The arugula topping is a basic version, but you can get more creative and add halved grape tomatoes, thinly sliced radish, or shaved carrot or fennel and make it a salad party on top of your pizza.

IN THE GLASS: Vermentino is a lively white wine from the Sardinia region of Italy. Similar to Sauvignon Blanc, it partners well with many dishes and can vary from grassy and herbaceous to fruity. All iterations are delightful; plus, it's usually inexpensive, making it a great bottle for a weeknight. Pizza night is a celebration, so let the kids in on the fun as well with a glass of apple-pomegranate blend and sparkling water.

Deviled Roast Chicken

with BACON and BRUSSELS SPROUT HASH

Devilishly good, this chicken dish is one of my family's favorite weeknight dinners. A little bacon crisps up and renders porky goodness to Brussels sprouts, while the mustard creates a flavorful but simple crispy topping on the chicken breasts. A splash of beer at the end pulls up any browned bits in the pan so that they end up where all that flavor belongs . . . on your plate and in your mouth.

4 slices bacon	*Kosher salt and freshly ground black pepper*
1 lb [455 g] Brussels sprouts	*2 Tbsp Dijon or grainy mustard*
1 small onion	*1½ lb [680 g] chicken cutlets*
2 garlic cloves	*⅓ cup [80 ml] beer, chicken or vegetable broth, or orange juice*
3 Tbsp olive oil	*2 Tbsp chopped fresh parsley*

1. Line a sheet pan with nonstick aluminum foil and place it in the oven. Preheat the oven to 425°F [220°C].

2. On a large cutting board, chop the bacon, halve and thinly slice the Brussels sprouts, slice the onion, and chop the garlic; transfer it all to a large bowl.

3. Toss the Brussels sprout mixture with 1 Tbsp of the olive oil, ¼ tsp salt, and a few grinds of pepper. Remove the sheet pan from the oven and spread the Brussels sprout mixture evenly in the hot pan. Roast until the sprouts begin to brown around the edges, about 15 minutes.

4. While the sprouts cook, combine the remaining 2 Tbsp olive oil with the mustard in a small bowl.

5. Sprinkle the chicken cutlets with salt and pepper and brush them with the mustard mixture.

6. Toss the sprouts with a spatula, and drizzle the beer over the top. Lay the cutlets on top of the sprouts and roast until the chicken is cooked through and the sprouts are tender, about 10 minutes.

7. Divide the chicken and vegetables among heated plates and sprinkle the tops with any juice remaining in the pan. Sprinkle with the parsley.

continued

It's that easy: *Slicing Brussels sprouts can be done on a mandoline, in a food processor with the slicing disk, or with a knife. I cut them in half through the stem end and then slice them thinly. You definitely get better with practice, so make sure your knife is sharp and start cutting. A time-saver is presliced Brussels sprouts, which can be found packaged in some grocery stores.*

EXTRA-HUNGRY KIDS? A salad of leaf lettuce, chopped apple, dried cranberries, walnuts, a splash of cider vinegar, and a glug of olive oil is all it takes.

ADULT TASTE BUDS? Top the kids' chicken breasts with some of the mustard mixture (or not) and then add 1 Tbsp of prepared horse-radish to the remaining mustard and spread over the adults' portions.

IN THE GLASS: The cool-weather vibe of this dish tells me to look for a light red wine here. Pick up a bottle of your favorite Beaujolais or perhaps a lighter rosé, which would be lovely if the weather is still a little on the warm side.

CUBAN-STYLE

Chicken Fricassee

You don't have to go to Cuba or even Miami to get great Cuban food. This fricassee has it all; loads of vegetables, citrus, and a touch of tomatoey sweetness make this stew a tropical bright spot on a cold and gloomy winter's day.

1 onion	*2 Tbsp raisins*
1 green bell pepper	*2 Tbsp honey, plus more if needed*
2 garlic cloves	*1½ lb [680 g] boneless, skinless chicken thighs*
5 new potatoes	*Seasoned salt or kosher salt and freshly ground black pepper*
10 pitted green olives	
1 orange	*2 Tbsp olive oil*
1 lime	*One 8-oz [227-g] can tomato sauce*
1 cup [240 ml] white wine	*½ cup [60 g] frozen peas*

1. On a large cutting board, chop the onion and bell pepper and mince the garlic; transfer it all to a medium bowl. Thinly slice the potatoes (do not peel) and chop the olives; set them aside. Grate the zest from the orange into a small bowl, then squeeze the orange juice into the bowl. Squeeze the lime juice into the bowl and add the wine, raisins, and honey.

2. Season the chicken with ½ tsp salt and a few grinds of pepper.

3. Heat a 4-qt [3.8-L] saucepan over medium-high heat and add the olive oil. When the oil shimmers, add the chicken and brown it for about 3 minutes (if

it sticks, give it another minute). Turn and brown the other side for another 3 minutes. Transfer to a plate. The chicken won't be cooked through at this point.

4. Add the onion, bell pepper, and garlic to the pan along with a sprinkle of salt and a few grinds of pepper. Sauté until the vegetables begin to soften, about 3 minutes. Add the chicken back to the pan along with the potatoes, olives, citrus mixture, and tomato sauce and bring to a simmer. Cover, reduce the heat, and simmer for 15 minutes to finish cooking the chicken and blend the flavors. Stir in the peas. Taste and add more salt, pepper, or honey if it needs it. You can also pick out the thighs at this point, cut them into smaller chunks, and return them to the pan.

5. Ladle the fricassee into heated bowls and serve hot, hot, hot.

It's that easy: *The honey in this dish is used to balance the acid in the citrus, wine, and tomato sauce. Without it, the sauce can taste a little sharp. If the flavor is too acidic when you taste the stew, add a little more salt and taste again. If that doesn't fix it, add a touch more honey and taste again. You'll soon get the hang of balancing tart flavors with sugar and salt.*

EXTRA-HUNGRY KIDS? Crumbled plantain chips make a terrific, crunchy topping.

ADULT TASTE BUDS? This is a fairly adult dish but if you want to zing it up, add some Cuban mojo sauce to the adult portions.

IN THE GLASS: Tempranillo usually goes well with Cuban flavors and this dish is no exception. Look for a bottle of Vega Sindoa Tempranillo for soft tannins, blackberry fruit, and a long finish. For the kids, serve an acai blend with coconut water.

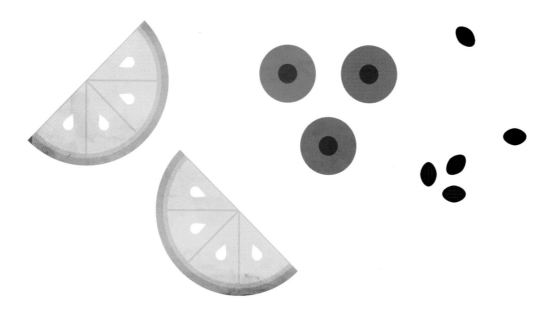

Orange Chicken Stew

with RED PEPPER and SWEET POTATOES

I've been making a version of this stew to rave reviews for over thirty years. I call it one of those "little black dress" recipes because depending on what you pair it up with, it makes an easy weeknight meal for the family, yet is impressive enough to serve to company. I've kept it simple here with steam-in-the-bag rice, but if you're celebrating a nice report card or a victory in the backstroke, this dish is amazing over Spring Mushroom and Pea Risotto (page 31) or polenta with a simple green salad on the side.

1 onion	*2 Tbsp olive oil*
1 red bell pepper	*1 tsp dried thyme*
2 carrots	*1 cup [240 ml] chicken broth*
1 celery stalk	*½ cup [120 ml] orange juice*
2 sweet potatoes	*¼ cup [10 g] chopped fresh flat-leaf parsley*
1½ lb [680 g] boneless, skinless chicken thighs	*Two 8- to 10-oz [227- to 283-g] bags frozen precooked brown rice*
Kosher salt and freshly ground black pepper	

1. On a large cutting board, chop the onion and bell pepper, peel and thinly slice the carrots and celery, and cut the potato into 1-in [2.5-cm] chunks. As you work, transfer the vegetables to a bowl.

2. Sprinkle the chicken with ½ tsp salt and a few grinds of pepper.

3. Heat a 12-in [30.5-cm] skillet over medium-high heat and add the olive oil. When the oil shimmers, add the chicken to the pan and brown it for about 3 minutes (if it sticks, give it another minute). Turn

and brown the other side for 3 to 4 minutes and transfer it to a plate. The chicken will not be cooked through at this point.

4. Add the bowl of vegetables, the thyme, a sprinkle of salt, and a few grinds of pepper to the pan and sauté until they begin to soften, about 4 minutes. Return the chicken to the pan along with the broth and juice and bring to a boil. Cover, reduce the heat to low, and simmer for 20 minutes or until the chicken and vegetables are tender. Scoop the chicken from the pot, raise the heat to medium-high, and cook the liquid and vegetables for another 3 to 4 minutes to reduce the liquid and increase the flavor. While the liquid reduces, cut or shred the chicken into bite-size pieces. Return the chicken to the pot along with half the parsley. Taste and add more salt or pepper if it needs it.

5. Cook the rice according to the package directions.

6. Divide the warm rice among shallow heated bowls, ladle the chicken stew over the rice, sprinkle with the remaining parsley, and serve.

It's that easy: *I like to brown chicken and meat before adding liquids in braises and stew recipes because I think the browned bits add flavor to the whole, but if you are in a super hurry and don't have time, sauté the vegetables for a few minutes, add the raw, seasoned chicken along with the liquids, and cook for 25 minutes instead of 20. The stew will still be very good and you've just saved yourself a little hands-on time.*

 EXTRA-HUNGRY KIDS? Add a couple of chopped zucchini or summer squash along with the vegetables.

 ADULT TASTE BUDS? A sprinkle of capers and Kalamata olives will add pops of saltiness to balance the sweetness of the orange-flavored sauce.

 IN THE GLASS: The orange and sweet potato make this stew a little sweet, so the wine should have a touch of residual sweetness. Look for a bottle of Riesling from Chateau St. Michelle for a wine that checks all the boxes.

Chicken Thighs

with SAUSAGE, RED BEANS, *and* RICE

This one is a little bit Cajun and a little bit Spanish. The combo of chicken and sausage, colorful kidney beans, carrots and pepper, and a racy Cajun seasoning feels like the bayou. Add shrimp and your taste buds will start making you think of paella.

1 onion

1 green bell pepper

2 garlic cloves

1 carrot

1 lb [455 g] boneless, skinless chicken thighs

Seasoned or kosher salt and freshly ground black pepper

1 Tbsp olive oil

8 oz [230 g] mild Italian sausage links

1 Tbsp Cajun seasoning or a blend of dried thyme, oregano, paprika, and cayenne pepper

One 15-oz [425-g] can kidney beans, drained and rinsed

One 15-oz [425-g] can diced tomatoes with juice

1 cup [240 ml] chicken broth

1 cup [130 g] instant brown rice

1. On a large cutting board, chop the onion, bell pepper, and garlic and peel and thinly slice the carrot. As you work, transfer the vegetables to a medium bowl.

2. Cut the chicken into bite-size pieces and season with 1/2 tsp of salt and a few grinds of pepper.

3. Heat a 12-in [30.5-cm] skillet over medium-high heat and add the olive oil. When the oil shimmers, add the chicken and brown it for about 3 minutes (if it sticks, give it another minute). Turn and brown the other side for another 3 minutes. Crumble the sausage and add to the pan with the vegetables and add the Cajun seasoning; cook, stirring and

breaking up the sausage every now and then, until the vegetables begin to soften, about 4 minutes.

4. Stir in the beans, tomatoes, and broth and 1/2 tsp salt and bring to a boil. Cover, reduce the heat to low, and cook for about 5 minutes to develop the flavors and soften the vegetables.

5. Stir in the rice, pressing down so that it's submerged in the liquid. Cover and continue to cook until the rice, meat, and vegetables are tender, about 15 minutes. Taste and season with more salt, pepper, or Cajun seasoning if it needs it.

6. Divide the stew among heated plates and serve hot.

ONE PAN, WHOLE FAMILY

It's that easy: *Cajun seasoning is definitely worth having in your spice cupboard. It has a little heat and usually contains paprika, celery seed, garlic, basil, white pepper, cayenne, thyme, and parsley. Look for it on the grocery shelf with the other spice and herb blends and add it to burgers, stews, and chilis for an easy flavor boost.*

 **EXTRA-HUNGRY KIDS?** Add 6 oz [170 g] shrimp with the rice and make it a version of paella.

ADULT TASTE BUDS? Top adult portions with chopped green olives, green onion, and Louisiana hot sauce.

IN THE GLASS: A red Côtes du Rhône Villages is my choice. It's easy to find great everyday bottles at reasonable prices, and there is such a variety of flavors and styles among the wineries that there's something for everyone to like. For spice, strawberry, and a long finish, look for a bottle from Familles Perrin Côtes du Rhône Villages. Pour the kids a glass of half apple-cherry blend and half sparkling water.

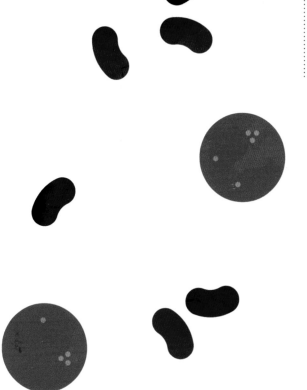

Chicken and Swiss Chard

in CIDER-CREAM SAUCE

It's so nice to sit down to a special dinner on a weeknight. And by special, I mean a meal that's good enough to serve company on a Saturday night. Lovely greens, mushrooms, and the simplest cider sauce this side of France accompany chicken thighs tender enough to make Julia Child swoon. I'm sure she smacked her lips many times over a dish such as this, and so will you.

1 onion	*2 Tbsp olive oil*
1 garlic clove	*¼ cup [60 ml] apple cider or apple juice*
1 bunch Swiss chard	*½ cup [120 ml] heavy cream*
8 oz [230 g] cremini or button mushrooms	*½ lemon*
1½ lb [680 g] boneless, skinless chicken thighs	*2 Tbsp chopped fresh flat-leaf parsley*
Kosher salt and freshly ground black pepper	

1. On a large cutting board, chop the onion and garlic; transfer them to a medium bowl.

2. Remove the ribs from the chard leaves, chop them, and add them to the bowl. Chop the leaves, trim and slice the mushrooms, and set them aside in separate piles.

3. Sprinkle the chicken with ½ tsp salt and a few grinds of pepper.

4. Heat a 12-in [30.5-cm] skillet over medium-high heat and add 1 Tbsp of the olive oil. When the oil shimmers, add the chicken and brown it, about 3 minutes (if it sticks, give it another minute). Flip it over and brown the other side, another 3 minutes. Transfer the chicken to a plate. It won't be cooked through at this point.

5. Add the remaining 1 Tbsp olive oil, the onion mixture, mushrooms, ½ tsp salt, and a few grinds of pepper to the pan and sauté until they begin to soften, about 3 minutes. Add the chard leaves and cook until they wilt, about 2 minutes. Add the cider and nestle the chicken into the vegetables. Cover, reduce the heat to low, and simmer for 5 minutes.

continued

Add the cream and cook, uncovered, until the chicken is cooked through and the sauce is reduced, about 5 minutes. Squeeze a few drops of lemon juice over it all. Taste and season with more salt and pepper if it needs it.

6. Divide the chicken and vegetables among heated plates and sprinkle with the parsley. Serve hot.

It's that easy: *I do love flavorful chicken thighs, but if you'd like to supplant them with breasts, that is your call. The cooking time will be about the same as long as the breasts aren't super big and thick. If they are thick, just slice the breasts in half horizontally, making them thinner, and proceed with the recipe.*

EXTRA-HUNGRY KIDS? Add a few diced apples along with the onion mixture and serve with precooked frozen brown rice or pasta.

ADULT TASTE BUDS? Serve the children's portions, then stir a Tbsp of apple brandy into the saucy vegetables in the pan.

IN THE GLASS: This creamy dish is looking for a crisp, dry Chenin Blanc. South Africa has many to choose from in the weeknight price range. Look for a bottle from Mulderbosch or Bellingham.

Chicken Thighs

with BALSAMIC BARBECUE SAUCE and CORN ON THE COB

If you haven't yet discovered the joys of boneless, skinless chicken thighs, this is the recipe to take you there. Juicy and so much more flavorful than breast meat, they taste great slathered with this addictive, tangy sauce. It's definitely worth the few minutes it takes to mix it up, but if you are super pressed for time, use your favorite bottled barbecue sauce instead. This dish works really well cooked on the grill too, which makes it ideal for hot summer evenings.

4 ears corn

3 Tbsp unsalted butter, softened

½ tsp Montreal steak seasoning, plus more for sprinkling

Freshly ground black pepper

1½ lb [680 g] boneless, skinless chicken thighs

1 Tbsp olive oil

2 garlic cloves

¼ cup [65 g] ketchup

2½ Tbsp balsamic vinegar

1½ Tbsp honey

1 Tbsp soy sauce

Store-bought potato salad or coleslaw

1. Line a sheet pan with aluminum foil and place it in the oven. Preheat the oven to 425°F [220°C].

2. Husk the corn; spread with the butter, a sprinkle of steak seasoning, and a few grinds of pepper; and wrap each ear individually with aluminum foil. Season the chicken thighs with ½ tsp steak seasoning.

3. Remove the sheet pan from the oven and arrange the thighs on one side of the hot pan. Drizzle them with the olive oil. Lay the corn on the other end of the pan and roast until the chicken registers 165°F [75°C] on an instant-read thermometer, about 20 minutes. (Or you can grill the chicken thighs 5 minutes per side on a medium-high grill. The same amount of time works for the corn, turning it once or twice.)

4. While the chicken and corn roast, mince the garlic and combine with the ketchup, vinegar, honey, and soy sauce in a medium bowl.

5. Brush the chicken with the glaze and return it to the oven for another 5 minutes. Brush again when you take it out of the oven. (If grilling, brush the chicken with the sauce a minute or so before removing it and then again just before serving.)

continued

WINNER, WINNER, CHICKEN DINNER

73

6. Serve the chicken and corn with coleslaw and extra sauce on the side.

It's that easy: *Prepare a double batch of chicken thighs and breast meat if you're cooking on the grill. That way you have ready-to-go chicken to top a simple green salad for the next night's dinner, no cooking required.*

EXTRA-HUNGRY KIDS? Throw a few more ears of corn in the oven. It's okay if they don't fit on the pan. Just lay them on the oven rack seam side up so that the butter doesn't escape.

ADULT TASTE BUDS? Sprinkle your corn with a little lime juice and Cotija cheese, a Mexican cheese similar to Parmesan, which you can use if you have trouble finding Cotija.

IN THE GLASS: An IPA from Fat Tire or your favorite local brewery will go down smooth like it's the weekend. Watermelon juice is perfect for the kids.

Chicken Sliders

with CHIPOTLE SLAW

Who needs a giant sandwich when a little one can pack this much flavor? It's amazing how a few minutes in a flavorful marinade can make such a difference in everyday chicken thighs. The spicy slaw is my favorite topping for sliders and burgers alike—and don't forget the pickles. Sweet or sour, they add crunch and a tart punch to these small-in-size but big-in-flavor sliders.

3 garlic cloves	*3 cups [180 g] packaged coleslaw mix*
2 Tbsp olive oil	*⅓ cup [80 g] mayonnaise*
1 Tbsp Worcestershire sauce	*3 Tbsp chopped fresh cilantro*
2 tsp chili powder	*1 Tbsp honey*
Kosher salt and freshly ground black pepper	*1 Tbsp fresh lime juice, plus more if needed*
8 to 10 boneless, skinless chicken thighs	*8 to 10 slider rolls, toasted*
½ to 1 tsp chipotle in adobo sauce	*Pickle slices (sweet or sour)*
1 green onion	*Your favorite condiments, such as mayo, mustard, and ketchup*

1. On a large cutting board, mince the garlic; transfer it to a large bowl. Stir in the olive oil, Worcestershire, chili powder, ½ tsp salt, and a few grinds of pepper. Add the chicken and toss to mix and coat with the marinade. Set aside at room temperature (it will absorb flavors more quickly on the counter, but if you are going to delay cooking for longer than 1 hour, refrigerate until ready to cook).

2. Mince the chipotle pepper finely and slice the green onion, including the white and tender green parts. Transfer to a large bowl and add the coleslaw mix, mayonnaise, cilantro, honey, lime juice, a sprinkle of salt, and a few grinds of pepper. Stir to combine, then taste and season with more salt, pepper, chipotle, or lime juice if it needs it. Refrigerate until ready to serve.

3. Fire up the grill to medium-high heat or preheat the broiler with an oven rack in the second-highest position. Remove the chicken from the marinade, pat it dry, and sprinkle with salt and a few grinds of pepper.

4. Grill the chicken thighs until they register 165°F [75°C] on an instant-read thermometer, about 5 minutes on the first side and about 4 minutes on the second side. Or place the thighs on a sheet pan and broil for about 6 minutes on each side.

5. Toast the rolls on the grill or under the broiler. They will take about 1 minute or less to toast, so watch that they don't burn.

6. Serve the chicken on the toasted slider rolls topped with the chipotle slaw, pickles, and the condiments of your choice.

It's that easy: *If you have the time, marinate the chicken thighs in the refrigerator for at least 2 and up to 4 hours. They'll be even juicier and more flavorful the longer rest they have in the garlicky, spicy marinade. By the way, chipotle is pretty spicy, so if you have heat-sensitive diners, add it sparingly.*

EXTRA-HUNGRY KIDS? Chips are the answer here, whether potato chips or corn chips accompanied by salsa. The salt and crunch are terrific with the sliders. You could also top the kids' chicken with a slice of American cheese at the last moment of cooking.

ADULT TASTE BUDS? The chipotle is quite adult already so you might separate out the adult slaw portion and add the hot stuff more liberally. There's also the option of topping the adult sliders with a cool blue cheese, which pairs beautifully with the spicy slaw.

IN THE GLASS: Dr. Konstantin Frank Semi Dry Riesling has just the right amount of sweet to counter the spiciness of the slaw on these sliders. This is one of those times a wine from the Finger Lakes in upstate New York really shines.

Drumsticks

with BARBECUE GLAZE *and* CONFETTI CORN

Chicken breast meat has been the king of the chicken coop for far too long. Legs are so much more flavorful (and less expensive!), with a lovely mix of dark and light meat intertwined. Plus, drumsticks are easy to hold on to while digging your teeth into that juicy barbecue-slathered meat. Accompanied by a colorful confetti of yellow corn, black beans, and red pepper bathed in a touch of cream, this meal is like a summer day on a plate. *Viva la* drumsticks!

8 chicken drumsticks	*1 garlic clove*
Seasoned or kosher salt and freshly ground black pepper	*½ cup [120 ml] barbecue sauce*
1 Tbsp olive oil	*1 tsp ground cumin*
1 onion	*One 15-oz [425-g] can black beans, drained and rinsed*
1 red bell pepper	*2 cups [280 g] frozen corn, thawed*
2 green onions	*¼ cup [60 ml] half-and-half*

1. Preheat the oven to 425°F [220°C].

2. Season the drumsticks with ½ tsp salt and a few grinds of black pepper.

3. Heat a 12-in [30.5-cm] ovenproof skillet over medium-high heat and add the olive oil. When the oil shimmers, add the chicken to the pan and cook for about 10 minutes, browning the drumsticks on all sides. Transfer the pan to the oven and roast for 10 minutes. The chicken won't be done cooking at this point.

4. While the chicken is in the oven, on a large cutting board, chop the onion and bell pepper, slice the green onions, and mince the garlic. Set aside in separate piles.

5. Transfer the drumsticks to a plate and brush with the barbecue sauce. Return the hot pan to medium-high heat (careful of the handle) and add the onion, garlic, bell pepper, and cumin to the pan. Sauté until the onion softens, about 2 minutes. Stir in the black beans, corn, half-and-half, and ½ tsp salt and bring to a simmer. Top with the chicken and return to the oven for another 5 minutes to finish cooking (the drumsticks should register 165°F [75°C] on an instant-read thermometer). Brush the drumsticks again with the barbecue sauce.

6. Divide the chicken and vegetables among heated plates. Sprinkle with the green onions and serve hot with more barbecue sauce on the side.

It's that easy: *There are countless barbecue sauces to choose from. Cruise down the condiment aisle and try something new every now and then. That's how you find a new favorite. Or if you have the time, make the balsamic barbecue sauce on page 73. That way you can fine-tune the ingredients to your personal tastes.*

EXTRA-HUNGRY KIDS? A colorful salad of chopped watermelon, crumbled feta cheese, a drizzle of balsamic, and a glug of olive oil is a cool and refreshing side dish.

ADULT TASTE BUDS? Douse the adults' leg portions with barbecue sauce with a little bourbon in it, or just add 1 Tbsp bourbon to the adult portion of barbecue sauce.

IN THE GLASS: This is barbecue after all, so beer is king, but sangria would also be a great option. It's a little fruity, which matches up with the sauce; plus, it's just delicious to sip on long after dinner is done. Kids love a blend of peach nectar and sparkling water. Don't forget a fun straw.

START TO FINISH
45 minutes
. . .
HANDS-ON TIME
15 minutes
. . .
SERVES
4
. . . .

Honey-Chipotle Chicken

with ROOT VEGETABLES

Every now and then I just love a chicken drumstick, and so do most kids, especially when they're served with sweet and spicy sauced carrots and parsnips. The citrusy sauce, smoky with chipotle chili, is just perfect.

5 medium carrots, about 12 oz [340 g]	*1 Tbsp olive oil*
5 medium parsnips, 12 oz [340 g]	*1 Tbsp honey*
1 small red onion	*1 tsp chili powder*
1 canned chipotle chile in adobo	*Kosher salt and freshly ground black pepper*
2 garlic cloves	*8 to 10 chicken drumsticks*
1 orange	*2 Tbsp chopped fresh cilantro*
1 lime	

1. Line a sheet pan with aluminum foil and place it in the oven. Preheat the oven to 425°F [220°C].

2. On a large cutting board, peel the carrots and parsnips, halve them lengthwise, and cut into 1-in [2.5-cm] pieces; transfer them to a large bowl. Cut the onion into 1-in [2.5-cm] pieces and add it to the bowl. Mince the chipotle chile and garlic and set aside.

3. Grate the zest from the orange into a small bowl, then squeeze the orange juice into the bowl. Cut the lime in half and squeeze the juice from one half into the bowl. Add the chipotle chile, garlic, olive oil, honey, chili powder, 1/2 tsp salt, and a few grinds of pepper and mix to combine well.

4. Season the chicken legs with salt and pepper, add them to the large bowl of vegetables, add the orange juice mixture, and toss it all together until the vegetables and chicken are evenly coated. Arrange the chicken and vegetables on the prepared sheet pan, chicken on one side and veggies on the other, spreading them out so that they cook evenly. Season again with salt and pepper.

5. Roast the chicken and vegetables for 30 minutes or until the chicken legs register 165°F [75°C]. Squeeze the remaining lime half over all.

6. Divide the chicken and vegetables among heated plates, sprinkle with the cilantro, and serve.

It's that easy: *Chipotle chiles are not for everyone and if you have some heat-sensitive tablemates, just substitute 3 Tbsp ketchup for the chipotle. It will still be delish.*

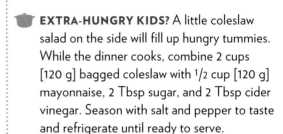

EXTRA-HUNGRY KIDS? A little coleslaw salad on the side will fill up hungry tummies. While the dinner cooks, combine 2 cups [120 g] bagged coleslaw with 1/2 cup [120 g] mayonnaise, 2 Tbsp sugar, and 2 Tbsp cider vinegar. Season with salt and pepper to taste and refrigerate until ready to serve.

ADULT TASTE BUDS? This is already a fairly adult meal as is, but you could always add a creamy blue cheese sauce to top the chicken and vegetables. Mix 1/4 cup [60 g] sour cream with 2 Tbsp mayonnaise and 3 Tbsp crumbled blue cheese.

IN THE GLASS: Spicy and beer just go together. An IPA from Crooked River Brewing or one from your local brewery would be just right.

Pasta Salad

with CHICKEN, GRAPES, *and* WALNUTS

Pasta salad makes a terrific summer meal. This one is loaded with vegetables and fruit, herbs, and cheese with an oniony walnut oil vinaigrette straight from the south of France. Picture yourself picnicking with your family on a blanket under the trees in your backyard tonight, nibbling this pasta salad from paper plates. Now you're getting the picture.

8 oz [230 g] rotini pasta	1 celery stalk
Kosher salt and freshly ground black pepper	12 oz [340 g] seedless red grapes
8 oz [230 g] green beans, trimmed	1 pear
1/2 shallot	2 1/2 cups [340 g] shredded rotisserie chicken
1 garlic clove	1/2 cup [60 g] crumbled feta cheese
2 Tbsp cider vinegar	1/4 cup [10 g] chopped fresh mint
1 Tbsp grainy Dijon mustard	1/4 cup [10 g] chopped fresh flat-leaf parsley
1/3 cup [80 ml] walnut oil or olive oil	1 baguette
2 handfuls arugula	Unsalted butter, softened
1/4 cup [30 g] chopped walnuts	

1. Fill a 4-qt [3.8-L] saucepan with water, cover, and bring it to a boil. Add the pasta and 2 tsp salt and cook for 5 minutes. Add the green beans and cook until the pasta is al dente and the beans are tender, about 4 minutes.

2. While the pasta cooks, on a large cutting board, mince the shallot and garlic. Transfer them to a large bowl. Add the vinegar, mustard, a sprinkle of salt, and a few grinds of pepper and stir to dissolve the salt. Whisk in the walnut oil and set aside.

3. Drain the pasta and green beans and transfer them to the bowl of dressing. Toss until well combined. Chop the arugula and add it to the bowl. Add the walnuts. Thinly slice the celery, halve the grapes, and peel and dice the pear, and stir them into the pasta. Add the chicken, feta cheese, mint, and parsley and toss to combine well. Taste and add more salt and pepper if it needs it.

4. Serve the salad at room temperature with bread and butter.

It's that easy: *Walnut oil is light, nutty flavored, and perfect for making vinaigrettes. Keep it in the fridge after opening and use it up quickly as it can go rancid fast.*

EXTRA-HUNGRY KIDS? Add another cup of shredded chicken to the salad to amp up the protein.

ADULT TASTE BUDS? Separate the adult portions before adding the feta cheese and sprinkle the adult plates with Roquefort or another blue cheese.

IN THE GLASS: A crisp, dry white like Assyrtiko from Santorini, Greece, takes this summer salad to the Aegean and back. Pink lemonade and sparkling water are made for drinking in the summer shade. Garnish the kids' glasses with a lemon slice.

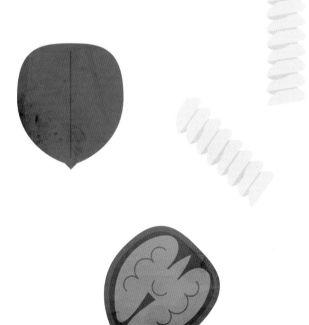

START TO FINISH
45 minutes
· · ·
HANDS-ON TIME
35 minutes
· · ·
SERVES
4

Tandoori Chicken

with SPICED CAULIFLOWER

This yogurt-and-spice-marinated chicken is traditionally cooked in a tandoor, a cylindrical clay oven that cooks food at a very high temperature. Since we don't have time on a weeknight to marinate chicken and we don't have tandoors, we can simply slather chicken with spices, cook it in a hot oven, and dress it with yogurt sauce and achieve pretty close to the same flavors. Garam masala is a spice that's aromatic and sweet and the yogurt sauce counters with its refreshing tartness. With ginger-spiced roasted cauliflower on the side, this weeknight version of restaurant-style tandoori chicken really delivers.

1 head cauliflower	*Kosher salt and freshly ground black pepper*
1 small red onion	*4 boneless, skinless chicken breasts*
One 1-in [2.5-cm] knob fresh ginger	*2 Tbsp fresh lemon juice*
2 garlic cloves	*1/3 cup [45 g] raisins*
2 Tbsp vegetable oil	*1/2 cup [120 g] plain Greek yogurt*
1 Tbsp garam masala	

1. Line a sheet pan with aluminum foil and place it in the oven. Preheat the oven to 425°F [220°C].

2. On a large cutting board, chop the cauliflower into bite-size pieces; transfer to a large bowl. Slice the onion and peel and mince the ginger, and add to the cauliflower. Chop the garlic and add half to the cauliflower and the other half to a medium bowl. Toss the vegetables with 1 Tbsp of the vegetable oil, 1 tsp of the garam masala, 1/2 tsp salt, and a few grinds of pepper to mix well.

3. Remove the sheet pan from the oven and spread the vegetables out evenly on the hot pan. Roast for 10 minutes.

4. While the vegetables cook, make three diagonal cuts about 1/4 in [6 mm] deep in each chicken breast and add them to the bowl with the garlic. Add 1 Tbsp of the lemon juice, the remaining 1 Tbsp vegetable oil, remaining 2 tsp garam masala, 1/2 tsp salt, and a few grinds of pepper. Mix with your hands to coat the chicken well with the spice mixture.

continued

5. Remove the sheet pan from the oven, push the vegetables to one side of the pan, and arrange the chicken breasts on the other side. Sprinkle the chicken with a little more salt and return to the oven; cook until the cauliflower has browned and the chicken is cooked through, about 20 minutes.

6. While the chicken and cauliflower cook, put the raisins in a small bowl and add hot tap water to cover. Let stand until the raisins become plump, about 10 minutes. Drain the raisins and set aside.

7. Combine the remaining 1 Tbsp lemon juice with the yogurt, a sprinkle of salt, and a few grinds of pepper. Divide the vegetables and chicken among heated plates, dollop with the yogurt sauce, and sprinkle with the raisins. Serve hot.

It's that easy: *Garam masala is probably the most familiar Indian spice blend. It contains cinnamon, cloves, cardamom, coriander, pepper, and cumin among other spices, so it's a terrific time-saver to have a jar on hand if you enjoy the tastes of India. Lots of grocery stores now carry garam masala in the spice or international aisle and it's also very easy to order online, so make some space for it on your spice shelf. You'll use it all the time.*

EXTRA-HUNGRY KIDS? It's traditional to serve a tomato salad with this zesty chicken dish. Dress sliced tomatoes with lemon, olive oil, salt, and pepper.

ADULT TASTE BUDS? Add a few pinches of cayenne pepper to the yogurt sauce on the adults' portions. The heat is a nice partner to the sweet aromatics in the Indian spices.

IN THE GLASS: An unoaked Chardonnay from Toad Hollow makes this meal feel like a holiday. It's a little leaner than more buttery oaked Chardonnays, and lots of wine lovers (including me) think unoaked Chardonnays partner better with food.

Tuscan Chicken

with SUN-DRIED TOMATOES *and* MUSHROOMS

Italian food is one of America's favorite cuisines and dishes like this prove why that is so. It's got everything: chicken, beans, vegetables, rosemary, and *molto* Italian flavor. I love how the rosemary permeates the stew-like mixture and how the sun-dried tomatoes are little exclamation points of bright flavor. There are lots of ways to make this more complicated but, as with most Italian food, simple really is best.

1 onion	*4 boneless, skinless chicken breasts*
1 carrot	*Kosher salt and freshly ground black pepper*
1 celery stalk	*2 Tbsp olive oil*
4 oz [115 g] cremini or button mushrooms	*1 tsp Italian seasoning*
1 garlic clove	*One 15-oz [425-g] can cannellini beans, drained and rinsed*
½ cup [120 ml] white wine or chicken broth	*¼ cup [25 g] oil-packed julienned sun-dried tomatoes*
1 tsp balsamic vinegar	*1 sprig rosemary*

1. On a large cutting board, thinly slice the onion. Peel and thinly slice the carrot. Slice the celery and mushrooms thinly. As you work, transfer the vegetables to a bowl. Mince the garlic and add to the vegetables. Combine the wine, vinegar, and ¼ cup [60 ml] water in a measuring cup.

2. Pat the chicken dry and sprinkle with salt and a few grinds of pepper.

3. Heat a 12-in [30.5-cm] skillet over medium-high heat and add the olive oil. When the oil shimmers, add the chicken and sauté without moving it for 3 minutes. Turn the chicken (if it sticks give it another minute) and sauté the other side for 2 minutes. Transfer to a plate. It won't be cooked through at this point.

4. Add the bowl of vegetables, Italian seasoning, ½ tsp salt, and a few grinds of pepper to the hot pan. Sauté, stirring, until the vegetables begin to soften, about 4 minutes. Add the wine mixture, beans, tomatoes, and rosemary sprig and stir to combine.

continued

Nestle the chicken breasts into the beans and vegetables and bring to a simmer. Reduce the heat to low, cover, and simmer until the chicken is cooked through and the flavors have blended, about 12 minutes. Pull out the rosemary sprig and discard it. Taste and season with more salt and pepper if it needs it.

5. Serve the chicken on heated plates with the beans and vegetables on the side.

It's that easy: *You can also make this dish with boneless, skinless chicken thighs. Cut them up after cooking and stir them into the beans.*

EXTRA-HUNGRY KIDS? Drizzle a few slices of country-style bread with olive oil and toast them in your toaster. Rub with a clove of garlic while still hot and sprinkle with Parmesan cheese.

ADULT TASTE BUDS? Though not traditional, a scattering of feta cheese is delish.

IN THE GLASS: A Tuscan dish needs Tuscan wine. Sangiovese, anyone? The kids might like something Italian as well. How about white grape, cherry, and sparkling water?

Chicken Saltimbocca

with BROCCOLINI and COUSCOUS

Saltimbocca is an Italian dish of veal (usually), wrapped in prosciutto and sautéed in butter with fresh sage and lemon. I've adapted the original by using chicken cutlets and adding fresh broccolini and quick-cooking couscous to the pan to make this a super-simple one-pan meal. Saltimbocca translated literally means "jump in the mouth." This dish definitely has the spark of the original and so will you when you find out how quickly this delicious, Italian-inspired meal comes together. *Mangia!*

1 bunch broccolini	*8 to 10 large fresh sage leaves*
1 shallot	*2 Tbsp unsalted butter, plus more if needed*
1 lemon	*2 Tbsp olive oil*
1½ lb [680 g] chicken cutlets (8 to 10 cutlets)	*⅓ cup [80 ml] dry white wine*
Kosher salt and freshly ground black pepper	*1 cup [240 ml] chicken broth, plus more if needed*
8 to 10 thin slices prosciutto	*¾ cup [135 g] couscous*

1. On a large cutting board, trim and chop the broccolini and mince the shallot; set aside. Cut the lemon into wedges and set them aside.

2. Season each chicken cutlet with a light sprinkle of salt and a few grinds of pepper. Lay one slice of prosciutto on top of each cutlet and place a sage leaf in the center of the prosciutto. Insert a toothpick down through the sage, prosciutto, and cutlet and then up through the meat and sage to secure it.

3. Heat a 12-in [30.5-cm] skillet with a lid over medium-high heat and add 1 Tbsp of the butter and 1 Tbsp of the olive oil. When the fat is hot, add half

the chicken cutlets, prosciutto side down. Sauté until golden, about 2 minutes, and then flip them over and sauté until the chicken is firm and cooked through, about 2 minutes. Transfer the cutlets to a plate, pull out the toothpicks, and keep warm. Add the remaining 1 Tbsp butter and 1 Tbsp olive oil to the pan and cook the remaining cutlets in the same manner, transferring them to the plate.

4. Add the broccolini and shallot to the pan (add more butter if there's none left in the pan) and sprinkle with salt and pepper. Sauté the vegetables for 2 minutes. Add the wine and stir to deglaze the pan and bring up all the brown bits stuck on the bottom of the pan. The wine will bubble away in about 1 minute. Add the chicken broth and bring to a boil. Stir in the couscous, pushing it down into the liquid, top with the chicken, cover, and remove from the heat. Let sit undisturbed for 5 minutes so that the couscous absorbs the liquid in the pan.

5. Arrange the chicken on heated plates with the couscous and vegetables on the side. Serve with the lemon wedges for squeezing.

It's that easy: *One of the things I really like about substituting chicken for veal in this dish is that you don't have to pound the chicken cutlets to make them tender, saving you time on busy nights.*

EXTRA-HUNGRY KIDS? Chop a few tomatoes and toss with a splash of balsamic vinegar, a glug of olive oil, and a generous handful of chopped basil leaves.

ADULT TASTE BUDS? Chilled pickled vegetables like an Italian giardiniera serves as a simple side dish.

IN THE GLASS: I'd go for a deliciously affordable, food-friendly red such as Dolcetto d'Alba from the Piedmont region of Italy. Much like Beaujolais, it is best drunk young, has nice fruit, and is easy on the pocketbook.

Chicken Fingers

with SMASHED POTATOES and MEXICAN DIP

Kids aren't the only ones who like chicken fingers. Crispy on the outside and juicy on the inside, chicken fingers are delish, especially when paired up with smashed fingerling potatoes and a creamy Mexican dip. Making your own allows you to know everything that's inside—nothing but the good stuff.

1 lb [455 g] fingerling potatoes

1 Tbsp olive oil

Kosher salt and freshly ground black pepper

1 garlic clove

8 oz [230 g] sour cream

1/3 cup [100 g] red salsa

1/4 cup [20 g] shredded Mexican blend cheese

Juice of 1/2 lime

2 Tbsp minced fresh cilantro

1 1/2 lb [680 g] boneless, skinless chicken breasts

1 1/2 cups [90 g] panko bread crumbs

1. Line a sheet pan with nonstick aluminum foil and place it in the oven. Preheat the oven to 425°F [220°C].

2. In a large bowl, toss the potatoes with the olive oil and sprinkle with 1/2 tsp salt and a few grinds of pepper.

3. Remove the sheet pan from the oven and spread the potatoes out evenly on the hot pan. Roast for 15 minutes.

4. While the potatoes roast, on a large cutting board, mince the garlic; transfer to a large bowl. Make a Mexican dip by adding the sour cream, salsa, cheese, lime juice, cilantro, 1/2 tsp salt, and a

few grinds of pepper to the bowl with the garlic. Mix to combine well. Transfer about 1 cup [240 ml] of the dip to a small serving bowl and set aside.

5. On the cutting board, slice each chicken breast into six strips. Transfer them to the large bowl of dip and toss to coat them well. Pour the panko out onto a plate and dredge the chicken fingers in the crumbs, pressing to coat them completely, then return them to the cutting board. Sprinkle them with more salt and pepper.

6. Remove the sheet pan from the oven, push the potatoes to one side of the pan, and arrange the chicken strips on the other side so that they are not touching. Return the pan to the oven; cook until the chicken is browned and the potatoes are tender, about 15 minutes.

7. Smash the potatoes with the back of a fork and sprinkle with more salt and pepper if you like.

8. Divide the chicken fingers and smashed potatoes among heated plates and serve with the reserved dip.

It's that easy: *I've made these in three different ovens and they turned out differently each time. If, at the end of 15 minutes, the chicken isn't browned, transfer the potatoes to another plate and run the chicken fingers under the broiler for a minute to crisp them up. Then flip them over and broil them bottom side up for a minute as well. It's worth the extra minute of cooking to make them super crispy.*

EXTRA-HUNGRY KIDS? Serve salsa with chips on the side.

ADULT TASTE BUDS? Chop up a jalapeño to garnish the adults' plates. Careful; it's spicy!

IN THE GLASS: A bottle of crisp and refreshing Portuguese vinho verde is perfect with this meal. For the kids, limeade cut with sparkling water will hit the spot.

Fried Chicken Tenders

with CORN CAKES and HONEY

Crispy chicken tenders and corn cakes put me in a Southern frame of mind and make me want to say, "Y'all come to the table now, y'hear." It's a little bit like breakfast and a little bit like dinner and that makes it lots of fun for kids and adults alike. There's no chopping involved in this recipe, so for one of those nights when you're just brain dead it's easy to assemble, cook, and eat.

1½ lb [680 g] chicken tenders	½ cup [120 ml] whole milk
Kosher salt and freshly ground black pepper	½ cup [70 g] all-purpose flour
2 Tbsp Dijon mustard	½ cup [70 g] cornmeal
2 Tbsp mayonnaise	2 tsp baking powder
1 cup [140 g] cornflake crumbs	Vegetable oil
1 egg	Honey or maple syrup
One 15-oz [425-g] can creamed corn	

1. Preheat the oven to 200°F [95°C].

2. Season the chicken with ½ tsp salt and a few grinds of pepper.

3. In a large bowl, combine the mustard and mayonnaise. Add the chicken and toss to coat.

4. Pour the cornflake crumbs into a shallow bowl or plate. Dredge the chicken in the crumbs, patting so that they adhere, and transfer them to a large plate.

5. In a large bowl, beat the egg. Add the creamed corn, milk, flour, cornmeal, baking powder, and

¼ tsp salt and stir just until mixed. It should be the consistency of pancake batter.

6. Heat a 12-in [30.5-cm] skillet over medium heat and add 1 Tbsp vegetable oil. When the oil shimmers, add ¼ cup [60 ml] of the batter to make four or five little pancakes. Cook for about 2 minutes until little bubbles appear (just like pancakes). Flip them over with a thin-edged spatula and cook the other side for another 2 minutes. Transfer the cakes to a heatproof plate, cover, and keep warm in the preheated oven. Repeat with the rest of the batter, adding more oil as necessary.

continued

7. Add 1 Tbsp vegetable oil to the pan, raise the heat to medium-high, and, working in batches, cook the chicken tenders until browned on the bottom, about 2 minutes (careful not to overcrowd the pan or they won't brown). Flip them over and brown the other side, another 2 minutes. As you work, transfer the cooked tenders to a heatproof platter and keep warm in the oven with the corn cakes. Add more oil to the pan as necessary.

8. Serve the corn cakes on heated plates topped with chicken and drizzled with honey.

It's that easy: If you can't find chicken tenders, just slice boneless, skinless chicken breasts into fingers (six to eight fingers per breast). They may take a bit longer to cook because they'll be thicker.

EXTRA-HUNGRY KIDS? A little green vegetable would be a welcome addition to the plate. Microwave some frozen broccoli or green beans and serve them on the side.

ADULT TASTE BUDS? Serve a salad of spring greens and radish with a splash of lemon and a glug of olive oil. Skip the honey and top the corn cakes with sour cream.

IN THE GLASS: Chardonnay and corn are perfect partners, so drink up whatever you have left in the bottle from the weekend or open a bottle of Sonoma-Cutrer Sonoma Coast Chardonnay.

Chicken Pot Pie

ON THE FLY

On the nights of the monthly dinner dance at the Elks Club, my mom usually fed us kids frozen chicken pot pies for dinner. She'd pop them in the oven and then dash back to the bedroom to put on makeup and sparkly earrings. My brother, sister, and I would watch from the bed while Dad stepped into his tuxedo with the plaid cummerbund. The oven timer would ding and we'd race back to the kitchen, anxious to crack the crispy crust hiding chicken and vegetables nestled in a creamy sauce. Oh, yeah. We were really livin'.

Though I might not consider myself lucky to get a frozen pot pie today, I do still love the comforting combination of a rich sauce, chicken, and veggies topped with a buttery crust. The good news is, it isn't very hard to make a truly wonderful pot pie and it will be ready in less than one hour.

1 onion	*¼ cup [35 g] all-purpose flour*
4 carrots	*2 cups [480 ml] chicken broth*
1 celery stalk	*½ cup [60 g] frozen peas, thawed*
4 new potatoes	*2 Tbsp minced fresh parsley*
1¼ lb [570 g] boneless, skinless chicken breasts or a mix of breasts and boneless, skinless thighs	*1 tsp cider vinegar or lemon juice*
Kosher salt and freshly ground black pepper	*1 sheet frozen puff pastry, thawed but well chilled*
3 Tbsp unsalted butter	*1 Tbsp milk*
2 Tbsp minced fresh sage, or 1 tsp dried	

1. Preheat the oven to 425°F [220°C].

2. On a large cutting board, chop the onion. Peel the carrots and slice them thinly; thinly slice the celery and potatoes (do not peel). As you work, transfer the vegetables to a medium bowl.

continued

3. Cut the chicken into bite-size pieces and sprinkle with 1/2 tsp salt and a few grinds of pepper.

4. Heat a 12-in [30.5-cm] ovenproof skillet over medium-high heat and add the butter. When it's melted, add the chicken and cook, stirring, until almost cooked through, about 3 minutes. Add the bowl of vegetables and 1 1/2 Tbsp of the sage and cook until the vegetables begin to soften, about 3 minutes. Add the flour and cook, stirring, for 1 minute. Quickly stir in the chicken broth and continue to cook, stirring frequently, until the sauce thickens, about 4 minutes. Remove the pan from the heat and stir in the peas, parsley, and vinegar. Taste and adjust the seasoning with more salt and pepper if it needs it.

5. Lay the chilled puff pastry out on a lightly floured work surface and cut it into six or eight large squares. Lay them in the pan, piecing them together to cover the top of the pie patchwork style. Brush the pastry with the milk and sprinkle it with the remaining 1/2 Tbsp sage. Bake for 20 minutes or until the top is crispy and golden and the vegetables and chicken are tender.

6. Divide the pot pie among heated plates and serve hot.

It's that easy: For this dish to cook quickly, the potatoes must be cut very thinly so they will be cooked through when the dinner bell rings.

EXTRA-HUNGRY KIDS? Add 1/2 cup [70 g] thawed frozen corn along with the peas.

ADULT TASTE BUDS? If you have it, a sprinkle of truffle salt elevates this dish to master status.

IN THE GLASS: How about a lean Pinot Noir with this creamy, rich chicken pot pie? I'd be happy to see a bottle from A to Z Wineworks on my weeknight table and I think you would, too. The kids will enjoy a glass of pear and blueberry juice splashed with sparkling water.

START TO FINISH
45 minutes
. . .
HANDS-ON TIME
20 minutes
. . .
SERVES
4

SWEET-*and*-SOUR

Turkey Meatballs

with BROWN RICE

This classic dish gets mom's seal of approval—it combines ground turkey with zucchini and is served over healthy brown rice—and it still has the irresistible sweet-and-sour flavors kids of all ages really love. At the end of the meal all you'll see is empty plates.

1 zucchini	*1 Tbsp olive oil*
1 egg	*2 cups [480 ml] chicken broth*
¼ cup [15 g] panko bread crumbs	*One 15-oz [425 g] can tomato sauce*
¼ cup [60 ml] milk	*One 8-oz [227-g] can crushed pineapple with juice*
1 lb [455 g] ground turkey	*¼ cup [50 g] brown sugar*
Kosher salt and freshly ground black pepper	*¼ cup [60 ml] cider vinegar*
1 onion	*¼ cup [65 g] ketchup*
2 carrots	*1 tsp Italian seasoning*
1 green bell pepper	*1 cup [130 g] instant brown rice*
1 green onion	

1. Grate the zucchini into a large bowl (you should have about 1 cup [225 g]). In a small bowl, beat the egg slightly and add it to the zucchini. Add the panko and milk to the zucchini and let sit for a minute so the panko soaks up the milk. Add the turkey, ½ tsp salt, and a few grinds of pepper and mix gently with your hands. Be careful not to overmix or the meatballs with be dense and tough. Shape into golf ball-size meatballs and set aside on a large plate.

2. On a large cutting board, chop the onion, peel and thinly slice the carrots, and thinly slice the bell pepper, and set aside in one pile. Thinly slice the green onion and transfer it to a small bowl.

3. Heat a 12-in [30.5-cm] skillet over medium-high heat and add the olive oil. When the oil shimmers, add the onion, carrots, and pepper to the pan along with a sprinkle of salt and a few grinds of pepper. Cook until the vegetables begin to soften, about 4 minutes. Stir in the broth, tomato sauce, pineapple, brown sugar, vinegar, ketchup, and Italian seasoning and bring to a boil. Nestle the meatballs into the sauce, cover, reduce the heat to medium-low, and simmer the meatballs for 5 minutes. Gently stir the rice into the mixture and simmer until the rice is cooked and the meatballs are tender, about 15 minutes.

4. Serve on heated plates sprinkled with the sliced green onion.

It's that easy: *Utilizing instant brown rice means you can get a healthy weeknight dinner on the table in no time flat. It's precooked and then dried, so it's ready to eat in under 15 minutes cooking time instead of the usual 30 minutes, saving you precious time.*

EXTRA-HUNGRY KIDS? A green salad of romaine lettuce, grated carrot, a splash of lemon juice, and a glug of olive oil is a perfect healthy side for the kids.

ADULT TASTE BUDS? A splash of Sriracha on adult plates adds heat and mitigates some of the sweetness.

IN THE GLASS: Look for an off-dry Riesling from the Mosel region of Germany, such as Peter Lauer Barrel X Mosel Riesling.

Turkey Chili

with CHILES and BLACK BEANS

Years ago, my husband came home from a trip raving about this white chili he had. I've been trying multiple versions ever since and have come to the conclusion that there are about as many kinds of delicious chilis as there are cooks. This version is as simple as it gets but still delivers on flavor. Using two kinds of beans adds color and texture to what is often just a bowl of beige, and the salsa verde adds a tangy note I find irresistible.

1 onion

2 garlic cloves

One 15-oz [425-g] can cannellini beans, drained and rinsed

One 15-oz [425-g] can black beans, drained and rinsed

One 7-oz [200-g] can diced green chiles, drained

1 Tbsp olive oil

2 Tbsp chili powder

½ tsp dried thyme

Kosher salt and freshly ground black pepper

1 lb [455 g] ground turkey

3 cups [720 ml] chicken broth

1 cup [240 g] jarred salsa verde, plus more if needed

Queso fresco

Corn chips

1. On a large cutting board, chop the onion and mince the garlic. In a medium bowl, lightly mash the cannellini beans. Add the black beans and chiles to the bowl.

2. Heat a 4-qt [3.8-L] saucepan over medium-high heat and add the olive oil. When the oil shimmers, add the onion, garlic, chili powder, thyme, 1 tsp salt, and a few grinds of pepper and cook, stirring, until the onion begins to soften, about 2 minutes. Add the turkey, breaking it up with a spoon and cooking until it's no longer pink, about 3 minutes.

3. Add the chicken broth, beans and chiles, and salsa verde and bring to a boil. Reduce the heat to low and simmer for 15 minutes to allow the flavors to mingle. Taste and adjust with more salt, pepper, or salsa verde if it needs it.

4. Serve hot in heated bowls topped with crumbled queso fresco and corn chips.

ONE PAN, WHOLE FAMILY

It's that easy: *I like my chili to be thicker with some body to it, so I mash the white beans with the back of a fork or a potato masher, which releases their starch. You can skip this step, but I think it makes the dish heartier and more filling.*

 **EXTRA-HUNGRY KIDS?** Add more chips and salsa on the side.

ADULT TASTE BUDS? Add chopped green onion and avocado on top. If you're looking for heat, try chipotle chile powder or pickled jalapeños.

IN THE GLASS: *Cerveza, por favor.* My favorite beer is a Corona longneck but a Dos Equis is just as tasty. Pour sparkling cider for the kids. If you have paper umbrellas, now is the time to use them.

Stracciatella

with CHICKEN and CROUTONS

There is absolutely no easier soup to make than stracciatella. Italian mothers have been making it for their families for centuries and chances are you have the ingredients in your fridge and pantry as we speak. I've added a little chicken and brown rice here, which is not traditional, but it makes the soup a bit more filling—great for satisfying hungry tummies.

---

4 boneless, skinless chicken thighs

Kosher salt and freshly ground black pepper

1 Tbsp olive oil

6 cups [1.4 L] chicken broth

½ cup [65 g] instant brown rice

3 eggs

¼ cup [20 g] grated Parmigiano-Reggiano cheese

2 Tbsp minced fresh flat-leaf parsley

Pinch of cayenne

Store-bought croutons

---

1. Cut the chicken into small pieces and season with salt and a few grinds of pepper.

2. Heat a 4-qt [3.8-L] saucepan over medium-high heat and add the olive oil. When the oil shimmers, add the chicken to the pan and sauté, stirring every now and then, until browned, about 6 minutes.

3. Pour in the broth and rice, cover, and bring to a boil. Reduce the heat and simmer for 7 minutes, until cooked through.

4. While the soup cooks, beat the eggs, cheese, parsley, and cayenne in a bowl until combined.

5. Slowly drizzle the egg mixture into the simmering soup while gently stirring with a large spoon. Remove the pan from the heat and let sit for about 1 minute to let the egg finish cooking.

6. Ladle the soup into heated bowls and sprinkle with croutons. Serve hot.

ONE PAN, WHOLE FAMILY

It's that easy: *This dish is so simple that the best ingredients will really make it shine. I find that purchased organic broths taste best. This is also a good time to use real Parmigiano-Reggiano instead of the stuff in the can. I know you probably already have that green can in your pantry, but once you experience real Parmesan cheese you'll find the taste so superior that you'll never buy a can again.*

 **EXTRA-HUNGRY KIDS?** How about a salad of Boston lettuce, cucumber, and halved grape tomatoes with a splash of white balsamic and a glug of olive oil?

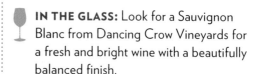 **ADULT TASTE BUDS?** Garnish the adult bowls with extra Parmesan, chopped fresh parsley, and a sprinkle of lemon zest.

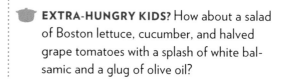 **IN THE GLASS:** Look for a Sauvignon Blanc from Dancing Crow Vineyards for a fresh and bright wine with a beautifully balanced finish.

Chicken Soup

with BLACK BEANS, CORN, and PEPITAS

Soup. Simple soup. It sustains, revives, strengthens, cures, and, most of all, fills you up on winter-chilled nights. A steaming bowl of soup is probably the most healthy and thrifty of meals, not to mention the fact that you can throw all those wondrous ingredients together in a pot and walk away to other chores while it simmers to deliciousness all by itself.

1 onion

2 carrots

1 celery stalk

2 garlic cloves

2 Tbsp olive oil

2 tsp chili powder

1½ tsp dried basil

6 cups [1.4 L] chicken broth

One 28-oz [800-g] can diced tomatoes with juice

One 4-oz [115-g] can chopped mild chiles with liquid

4 cups [560 g] shredded rotisserie chicken

One 15-oz [430-g] can black beans, drained and rinsed

2 cups [280 g] fresh or frozen corn

Kosher salt and freshly ground black pepper

¼ cup [35 g] roasted pepitas (pumpkin seeds)

¼ cup [10 g] chopped fresh cilantro

1. On a large cutting board, dice the onion, peel and thinly slice the carrots, thinly slice the celery, and mince the garlic.

2. Heat a 4-qt [3.8-L] saucepan over medium-high heat and add the olive oil. When the oil shimmers, add the onion, carrots, celery, and garlic and sauté until the vegetables are slightly softened, about 3 minutes. Add the chili powder and basil and stir for 1 minute. Add the broth, tomatoes, and chiles and bring to a simmer. Reduce the heat to low and simmer for 15 minutes.

3. Add the chicken, black beans, and corn and simmer for 5 minutes more. Season the soup with 1 tsp salt and a few grinds of pepper.

4. Ladle the soup into heated bowls, garnish each serving with a generous spoonful of pepitas and a sprinkle of cilantro and serve.

ONE PAN, WHOLE FAMILY

It's that easy: *Canned tomatoes, chiles, and black beans are easily added to the fresh onion, carrot, and celery (which one should always have in the fridge), chicken broth, dried basil, and chili powder from the pantry.*

EXTRA-HUNGRY KIDS? Add a can of drained garbanzo beans along with the black beans.

ADULT TASTE BUDS? Add a sprinkle of smoked paprika to the adult bowls.

IN THE GLASS: I like a glass of Beaujolais with this soup. Look for something floral and fruity from Georges Duboeuf or Joseph Drouhin.

Chicken Soup with Leeks

and WIDE NOODLES

No matter the season, it's the rare night my family is *not* excited to find chicken soup for dinner. It's one of their favorite meals. My trick to making really flavorful chicken soup quickly enough to serve on weeknights lies in simmering boneless, skinless chicken thighs and vegetables together in a flavorful chicken broth. This one-two punch results in a deeply rich soup that earns even Bubbe's seal of approval. I like using leeks in my soup, but if you only have an onion in the pantry, go ahead and use it.

2 leeks, trimmed and washed

3 carrots

1 celery stalk

1 lb [455 g] boneless, skinless chicken thighs

1 tsp dried thyme

Kosher salt and freshly ground black pepper

2 Tbsp unsalted butter or vegetable oil

8 cups [2 L] chicken broth

8 oz [230 g] dried wide egg noodles

1/2 cup [60 g] frozen peas, thawed

1/4 cup [10 g] chopped fresh flat-leaf parsley

2 Tbsp fresh lemon juice

2 Tbsp minced fresh chives

1. On a large cutting board, thinly slice the leeks. Peel and thinly slice the carrots. Thinly slice the celery. Transfer them to a large bowl. Cut the chicken thighs into bite-size pieces and season them with the thyme, 1/2 tsp salt, and a few grinds of pepper.

2. Heat a 4-qt [3.8-L] saucepan over medium-high heat and add the butter. When the butter is hot, add the chicken pieces and sauté them, without moving them, for about 3 minutes. Stir in the leeks, carrots, and celery and sauté until the vegetables begin to soften, about 4 minutes.

3. Add the chicken broth, 1 tsp salt, and a few grinds of pepper and bring to a simmer. Reduce the heat and simmer until the chicken is cooked and the flavors have blended, about 20 minutes.

4. Stir in the noodles and cook until tender, about 5 minutes. Stir in the peas, parsley, and lemon juice and taste, adding more salt and pepper if it needs it.

5. Ladle the soup into heated bowls and sprinkle with the chives. Serve.

continued

WINNER, WINNER, CHICKEN DINNER

It's that easy: *Leeks always seem to have a lot of grit trapped in their layers. The best way to get rid of it is to trim away the dark green parts and root end. Cut the leek in half lengthwise and hold it under running water, fanning the layers like a deck of cards.*

EXTRA-HUNGRY KIDS? Pick up some corn bread at the grocery bakery. It's so good crumbled into the soup.

ADULT TASTE BUDS? Serve the children's portions and stir a few tsp Thai red chili paste into the remaining soup in the pan. Top the adults' portions with chopped cilantro.

IN THE GLASS: Erath Pinot Blanc is loaded with apple, pear, and peach flavors with just the right amount of naughty to lighten up this very-good-for-you soup.

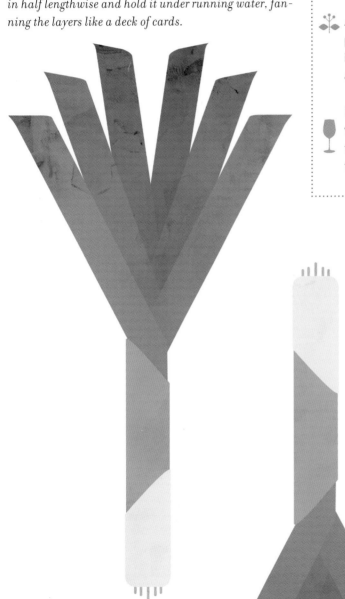

Tortilla Soup

with CHICKEN *and* SAUSAGE

You can spend a lot of time making a traditional tortilla soup, but why would you when this quick and easy version tastes so good? There are chunks of chicken and sausage in here to make it hearty, and the chips thicken the soup and add another layer of corny flavor. For me, the garnishes of avocado, cheese, and sour cream are mandatory and make this soup more than the sum of its parts.

1 onion	4 cups [960 ml] chicken broth
3 garlic cloves	One 15-oz [425-g] can fire-roasted diced tomatoes
2 limes	1/2 cup [70 g] frozen corn
1 lb [455 g] boneless, skinless chicken thighs	1/4 cup [10 g] chopped fresh cilantro
1 Tbsp chili powder, plus more if needed	Corn chips
1/2 tsp ground cumin	Grated Monterey Jack cheese
Kosher salt and freshly ground black pepper	Diced avocado
2 Tbsp olive oil	Sour cream
8 oz [230 g] mild Italian bulk sausage	

1. On a large cutting board, chop the onion and garlic. Transfer to a small bowl. Halve one lime, quarter the other, and set them aside.

2. Cut the chicken into bite-size pieces and sprinkle with the chili powder, cumin, 1/2 tsp salt, and a few grinds of pepper.

3. Heat a 12-in [30.5-cm] skillet over medium-high heat and add the olive oil. When the oil shimmers, add the chicken to the pan and cook for 3 minutes without moving it. Crumble in the sausage, and add the onion and garlic, a sprinkle of salt, and a few grinds of pepper. Cook, stirring every now and then, until the sausage is no longer pink and the onion has softened, about 4 minutes. Stir in the broth and tomatoes and bring to a boil. Reduce the heat to low and simmer until the chicken is tender and the flavors have blended, about 15 minutes. Add the corn and half the cilantro.

continued

WINNER, WINNER, CHICKEN DINNER

111

4. Squeeze the juice from a lime half into the soup. Taste, and add more lime juice, salt, pepper, or chili powder if it needs it.

5. Crumble a handful of corn chips into each heated bowl and ladle the hot soup over the top. Garnish the soup with cheese, avocado, sour cream, and a sprinkle of the remaining cilantro and serve with the lime quarters on the side for extra zing.

It's that easy: *Fire-roasted tomatoes really add extra oomph to this dish. If you can find them, buy a few extra cans and try them out in other recipes that call for diced tomatoes as well.*

EXTRA-HUNGRY KIDS? Add another 1/2 cup [70 g] corn to the pot.

ADULT TASTE BUDS? Top adult portions with a sprinkle of Cotija cheese and chipotle chile powder for a dash of cheesy heat.

IN THE GLASS: Light and refreshing, a Pacifico beer is the way to go. Make a tropical spritzer for the kids: combine orange juice, guava juice, and sparkling water. We save fun cocktail stirrers and pop them in the kids' drinks on special occasions. They love it.

CHAPTER

3

Let's Eat Meat

Tomato Pizza

with SPINACH, FRESH MOZZARELLA, *and* PEPPERONI

There is not a simpler pizza to make on the planet than this tomato and cheese pie topped with spinach and pepperoni. Obviously, the better the tomatoes, the better the pizza, but the layer of garlic and oil inspires even a not-so-great winter tomato to taste like, well, a tomato. The mozzarella and fresh basil topping is helped out by a scattering of Parmesan and spicy pepperoni in what just might be the perfect pie.

2 medium vine-ripe tomatoes

8 oz [230 g] fresh mozzarella cheese

2 garlic cloves

1 bunch fresh basil

1 lb [455 g] frozen pizza dough, thawed and out of the refrigerator for about 10 minutes

1 Tbsp olive oil

2 cups [40 g] baby spinach

Kosher salt and freshly ground black pepper

¼ cup [20 g] grated Parmesan cheese

6 oz [170 g] sliced pepperoni

1. If you have a pizza stone, place it on the bottom rack of the oven. If you don't have a stone, you can bake the pizza on a sheet pan. (It won't be as crispy on the bottom and may take a few more minutes to bake.) Preheat the oven to 450°F [230°C].

2. On a large cutting board, slice the tomatoes and mozzarella thinly and mince the garlic. Tear the basil leaves into small pieces, discarding the stems.

3. On a lightly floured surface, pat and stretch out the dough into a 16-in [40.5-cm] circle and place it on a sheet of parchment paper. Transfer the dough and parchment to a pizza peel or a rimless sheet pan. Drizzle the dough with the olive oil, rub

the garlic over the top with your fingers, and layer on the spinach, tomatoes, a few sprinkles of salt, a few grinds of pepper, the mozzarella, Parmesan, and pepperoni.

4. Slide the pizza, still on the parchment, onto the heated pizza stone or transfer the sheet pan to the oven. Bake until the bottom is crispy and the cheese has browned slightly, 10 to 15 minutes.

5. Slide the peel under the pizza to remove it from the stone or transfer the sheet pan to a wire rack. Scatter the basil over the pizza and let cool for about 5 minutes before cutting into wedges. Serve hot.

ONE PAN, WHOLE FAMILY

It's that easy: *I make it a point to slice tomatoes thinly when topping a pizza because each slice will be lighter, which makes it less floppy and easier to eat out of hand.*

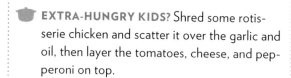 **EXTRA-HUNGRY KIDS?** Shred some rotisserie chicken and scatter it over the garlic and oil, then layer the tomatoes, cheese, and pepperoni on top.

ADULT TASTE BUDS? Lay down some roasted red pepper, patted dry, with the tomatoes on the adult portions.

IN THE GLASS: Let's stick with the Italian theme and go with a Sangiovese. Serve the kids a mocktail of sparkling water and cranberry juice.

Bacon Frittata

with BROCCOLI, RED BELL PEPPER, *and* CHEDDAR

Frittatas are my ace-in-the-hole dinner and this recipe is one of my favorites. Bacon really does make everything better and the vegetables cooked in bacon fat fill this veggie-packed frittata with even more porky goodness. Loaded with green broccoli and Cheddar cheese, leftovers (if you have any) are delicious for breakfast the next day.

One 12-oz [340-g] bag steam-in-the-bag frozen broccoli

7 eggs

Kosher salt and freshly ground black pepper

4 slices bacon

1 onion

1 red bell pepper

1 cup [80 g] shredded Cheddar, Colby Jack, or pepper Jack cheese

1. Preheat the broiler to high with the rack on the second-highest level.

2. Cook the broccoli in the microwave according to the package directions and drain any liquid.

3. In a medium bowl, whisk the eggs with 1/2 tsp salt and a few grinds of pepper.

4. On a large cutting board, chop the bacon, onion, and bell pepper and set aside in separate piles.

5. Heat a 12-in [30.5-cm] ovenproof skillet over medium-high heat and add the bacon. Cook until browned, about 4 minutes, and transfer the bacon to a paper towel-lined plate.

6. Add the onion, bell pepper, a sprinkle of salt, and a few grinds of pepper to the fat in the pan and sauté until tender, about 3 minutes.

7. Add the broccoli and toss until it's hot. Season again with a sprinkle of salt and pepper.

8. Add the bacon to the pan and toss to incorporate it evenly. Sprinkle the cheese over the top and pour the eggs evenly over the vegetables. Cover, reduce the heat to low, and cook for 2 minutes. Remove the lid, transfer the pan to the oven, and broil until firm and cooked through, 3 to 4 minutes. Watch that the top doesn't burn. Remove from the oven and let rest for 2 minutes before cutting. Serve hot on heated plates.

It's that easy: *When making a frittata, make sure that all the vegetables are tender and hot before adding the eggs and cheese. The eggs cook so fast that the vegetables won't have time to finish cooking once the eggs are poured in, so check them for tenderness and cook them another minute or so if you have any doubts.*

EXTRA-HUNGRY KIDS? Bulk this frittata up with a few extra eggs and more cheese.

ADULT TASTE BUDS? Frittata and hot sauce just go together. My favorite is Louisiana Hot Sauce. My husband's is Frank's. We probably have about six or seven other labels in the fridge and all are different. Find your favorite and you won't eat eggs without it.

IN THE GLASS: Cold and refreshing, a glass of lean, dry Codorniu Anna de Cava Brut Rose Champagne cuts through the richness of this dish with the flavors of peach, cherry, and pear. Pour the kids a glass of mixed cherry juice and limeade so they can join in the fun.

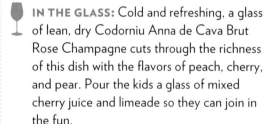

Ribollita with Ham

Ribollita is a classic Italian soup made with beans, water, vegetables, and bread. It's a vegetarian soup meant to feed hungry people when the cupboards were bare, and I admire that, but taking the basics of this soup and adding a little ham just makes it taste soooo much better. So, even though this isn't a classic rendition of ribollita, I'm sure it will make everyone at your table smile.

1 onion

1 carrot

1 celery stalk

2 garlic cloves

¼ cup [60 ml] olive oil

8 oz [230 g] chopped ham

Kosher salt and freshly ground black pepper

4 cups [960 ml] vegetable broth

One 15-oz [425-g] can cannellini beans, drained and rinsed

One 15-oz [425-g] can diced tomatoes with juice

1 sprig rosemary

5 oz [140 g] baby kale

4 to 6 slices country-style bread

Red pepper flakes (optional)

½ cup [40 g] grated Parmesan cheese

1. On a large cutting board, chop the onion. Peel and thinly slice the carrot, thinly slice the celery, and mince the garlic.

2. Heat a 4-qt [3.8-L] saucepan over medium-high heat and add 2 Tbsp of the olive oil. When the oil shimmers, add the onion, carrot, celery, garlic, ham, a sprinkle of salt, and a few grinds of pepper and cook, stirring occasionally, until the vegetables are tender, about 5 minutes.

3. Stir in the broth, beans, tomatoes, and rosemary sprig and bring to a boil. Reduce the heat to low,

partially cover, and simmer the soup for 10 minutes to finish cooking the vegetables and meld the flavors.

4. Pick out the rosemary sprig and stir in the kale. Simmer uncovered for another 5 minutes.

5. While the soup simmers, toast the bread in a toaster.

6. Taste the soup and season with more salt, pepper, or red pepper flakes.

ONE PAN, WHOLE FAMILY

7. Ladle the soup into heated bowls, top with a slice of bread, and drizzle with the remaining 2 Tbsp olive oil. Sprinkle with Parmesan. Slurp happily.

It's that easy: *If you'd like to make the soup heartier, mash up half of the cannellini beans with the back of a fork before adding them to the pot. It only takes a minute and creates a stick-to-your-ribs texture that I find irresistible.*

EXTRA-HUNGRY KIDS? Serve a little chunk of cheese on the side. I would choose Parmesan, but string cheese fills them up as well and they love to play with it.

ADULT TASTE BUDS? Spread your bread with store-bought tapenade before laying it in your soup. No tapenade in the house? Add a spritz of lemon zest for a little sunshine in your soup.

IN THE GLASS: Keep it Italian and serve this soup with a well-chilled Pinot Grigio.

Cheesy Mac

with SPINACH and HAM

I make mac and cheese on weeknights because that is when I really need something fabulous to get me through the midweek doldrums. I've even found a way to make it so that I don't have to cook the pasta separately! So come on. There's even spinach and ham inside. And cheese, glorious cheese.

1 onion	*3 Tbsp all-purpose flour*
1¼ cups [300 ml] milk	*8 oz [230 g] Cheddar or Jarlsburg cheese, shredded*
1 cup [240 ml] half-and-half	*1½ cups [360 ml] vegetable broth*
2 tsp Dijon mustard	*10 oz [280 g] elbow macaroni (about 2 cups)*
4 Tbsp [55 g] unsalted butter plus 1 Tbsp, melted	*4 oz [115 g] chopped ham*
5 oz [140 g] baby spinach	*½ cup [30 g] panko bread crumbs*
Kosher salt and freshly ground black pepper	

1. Preheat the oven to 400°F [200°C].

2. On a large cutting board, mince the onion. Combine the milk, half-and-half, and mustard in a measuring cup and set aside.

3. Heat a 12-in [30.5-cm] ovenproof skillet over medium-high heat and add 4 Tbsp butter. When the butter melts, add the onion and sauté until it softens, about 2 minutes, then add the spinach, ½ tsp salt, and a few grinds of pepper. Sauté until the spinach wilts, about 1 minute.

4. Stir in the flour and cook for 1 minute, stirring, then stir in the milk mixture, stirring constantly. Be sure to scrape up any flour stuck on the bottom of the pan. Continue to stir until the sauce thickens, about 2 minutes, and then stir in the cheese. Continue to stir until the cheese melts and then stir in the broth, macaroni, and ham. Make sure the pasta is submerged in the liquid, pressing it down. Cover the pan with an ovenproof lid and bake until the pasta is tender, about 20 minutes.

5. While the pasta bakes, stir together the panko and remaining 1 Tbsp melted butter with a fork.

continued

6. Remove the lid and sprinkle the panko topping over the pasta. Switch the oven setting to broil, return the pan to the second-highest rack, and broil the topping until browned, 1 to 2 minutes.

7. Serve the mac and cheese directly from the pan at the table so that it stays good and hot.

It's that easy: *You may think you don't need to buy panko. But you do. If you're not familiar with it, panko is crunchy Japanese bread crumbs and they are so much more delicious than that sawdust in a can masquerading as bread crumbs that you probably have in your pantry. Panko's larger crumbs add greater crunch, especially for crunchy coatings and toppings like this. Buy a bag or a box and use them whenever you would bread crumbs.*

EXTRA-HUNGRY KIDS? It's not likely, but if you're looking for something green, add a side of microwaved frozen peas or green beans.

ADULT TASTE BUDS? This is one meal adults and kids agree on, but if you need some relief from all the richness there's nothing like thinly sliced cucumbers splashed with white wine vinegar, a glug of olive oil, and a sprinkle of fresh dill.

IN THE GLASS: An off-dry Riesling from Jacob's Creek works perfectly with the rich cheese. The kids might like a mocktail of carrot juice, pineapple juice, and sparkling water.

START TO FINISH
35 minutes
...
HANDS-ON TIME
20 minutes
...
SERVES
4-6

Stovetop Lasagna

with SPINACH

The quest for weeknight meals usually leaves lasagna out of the game. Boiling noodles and cooking up sauce just isn't on my radar on a hectic weeknight. But lasagna is something my kids would *always* eat, and to be honest, my husband and I are rather fond of it as well. So I came up with a lasagna made in a skillet, on the stove, no boiling of noodles or separate pot of sauce required. I use no-boil lasagna sheets (which are genius) and mix the ricotta cheese in with the meat and tomato mixture (I am genius), eliminating the big assembly. There's a healthy bag of spinach in there as well (shhhh). The kids won't even notice because they'll be so busy gobbling up all that meaty, cheesy lasagna. Delicious lasagna with one-pan cleanup. I promise.

1 onion	*³⁄₄ cup [180 ml] beef broth*
2 garlic cloves	*¹⁄₂ cup [120 g] ricotta cheese*
1 Tbsp olive oil	*Red pepper flakes (optional)*
1 lb [455 g] ground meat loaf mix (beef, pork, and veal)	*6 no-boil lasagna noodles*
Kosher salt and freshly ground black pepper	*1 cup [80 g] shredded mozzarella cheese*
5 oz [140 g] baby spinach	*¹⁄₄ cup [20 g] grated Parmesan cheese*
1¹⁄₂ cups [360 ml] jarred marinara sauce	*¹⁄₄ cup [10 g] chopped fresh basil*

1. On a large cutting board, chop the onion and mince the garlic.

2. Heat a 12-in [30.5-cm] skillet over medium-high heat and add the olive oil. When the oil shimmers, add the onion and sauté until it begins to soften, about 1 minute. Add the garlic, meat loaf mix, 1 tsp salt, and a few grinds of pepper, breaking the meat into small pieces with a spatula as it cooks. Cook until the meat is no longer pink. Add the spinach in

two batches, turning with tongs until it wilts, about 1 minute. Stir in the sauce, broth, ricotta cheese, and red pepper flakes, if using. Stir and bring to a boil. Taste and adjust the seasoning with more salt, pepper, or pepper flakes. Remove from the heat.

3. Transfer two-thirds of the meat mixture to a medium bowl. Lay three of the noodles in the pan,

continued

breaking them up to fit so it covers the sauce left in the pan. Cover with half the sauce and the remaining three noodles. Top with the remaining sauce, pushing the noodles down into the sauce so that they are covered. Sprinkle with the mozzarella and Parmesan cheeses. Cover and return the pan to medium-low or low heat. Simmer until the noodles are tender, about 15 minutes.

4. Serve hot on heated plates sprinkled with basil.

It's that easy: Use a good jarred sauce here and the quality will show.

EXTRA-HUNGRY KIDS? There's always Italian bread and butter.

ADULT TASTE BUDS? An arugula salad with sliced cucumber, your favorite olives, a splash of balsamic vinegar, and a glug of olive oil would be a light counterpoint to the saucy, cheesy, pasta.

IN THE GLASS: Look for a Tuscan red or Chianti at your grocery store. If you have a wine guy or gal, ask them their advice. You might find a new favorite!

CLASSIC

Pasta Carbonara

Sophia Loren famously said, "I'd much rather eat pasta and drink wine than be a size zero." I think of her every time I make this dish. Rich, salty, creamy, and hot all the way from your mouth to your tummy, this dinner is perfect for when you feel a need to splurge on something fabulous.

3 garlic cloves	*Kosher salt and freshly ground black pepper*
8 slices bacon	*1 lb [455 g] fresh linguine*
2 oz [55 g] Parmigiano-Reggiano cheese, plus more for sprinkling	*1 Tbsp olive oil*
3 eggs	*¼ cup [10 g] minced fresh parsley*

1. Fill a 4-qt [3.8-L] saucepan with water, cover, and heat it over medium-high heat until it boils.

2. While the water comes to a boil, on a large cutting board, mince the garlic and transfer it to a small bowl. Chop the bacon. Grate the cheese into a small bowl. In a medium bowl, whisk the eggs with ¼ tsp salt and a few grinds of pepper.

3. When the water boils, add 1 Tbsp salt and the pasta to the pot. Stir once or twice to keep the pasta from sticking and cook a minute or so less than the package directs. Test the pasta by pulling out a piece and taking a bite. (It's important that the pasta isn't completely cooked at this point. It will still be a little chewy. Don't worry; the pasta will finish cooking in the sauce.)

4. Using a heatproof measuring cup, scoop out about ½ cup of the pasta water and whisk ¼ cup into the egg mixture, reserving the rest. Drain the pasta in a strainer in the sink and run cold water over it for a second just to stop the cooking. It should still be hot.

5. Return the empty hot pan to the heat and add the olive oil and chopped bacon. Cook until the bacon is crispy, about 3 minutes. Transfer the bacon with a slotted spoon to the egg mixture and remove the pan from the heat.

6. Add the garlic to the hot pan and cook it off the heat or until it is fragrant, about 20 seconds. It should sizzle. Return the drained pasta to the pan, return the pan to low heat, and toss the pasta in the hot fat for about 1 minute to reheat it. Quickly pour in the egg mixture, the cheese, half the parsley, and the remaining ¼ cup pasta water and toss to blend and finish cooking the ingredients thoroughly, about 1 minute. The egg should thicken into a sauce. Taste it for seasoning and add more salt and pepper if it needs it. Continue to toss for another minute over low heat if it isn't hot enough.

7. Heap the pasta onto heated plates, sprinkle with the remaining parsley and more cheese, and serve. Pasta has a tendency to cool off quickly when piled onto a cold plate, so be sure to heat the plates in the microwave for a minute or so to take the chill off.

It's that easy: Try to avoid the green can of cheese for this recipe. In a dish as simple as this one, good cheese makes all the difference and though it's an extra step, freshly grated is best. Look for individually wrapped chunks of Parmesan in the cheese bin section at your grocery. Authentic Italian Parmesan should have a dot matrix design on the rind spelling out "Parmigiano-Reggiano." If you can't find Parmigiano-Reggiano, then an authentic pecorino romano is a better bet than going with a cheaper Parmesan.

EXTRA-HUNGRY KIDS? A leaf lettuce salad tossed with a peeled and diced navel orange, a sprinkle of walnuts, a splash of cider vinegar, and a glug of olive oil is all you need.

ADULT TASTE BUDS? Shake some red pepper flakes over your portion. The heat adds a terrific dimension to the cheesy, rich pasta. If you have it, a drizzle of truffle oil is divine.

IN THE GLASS: Just about any medium-bodied red will do here, but if you're looking for perfection, this rich Italian dish calls out for a Chianti or Tuscan red. Sophia would approve.

Pork Chops

with SWEET POTATOES *and* APPLE GLAZE

Pork appears on our plates more often than red meat these days. It pairs up perfectly with the sweet potatoes and gingery pear roasted on the side, pleasing kids of all ages. If you haven't tried them, thicker pork chops are juicier than thinner cuts. You'll be amazed at the savory difference between a $^{1}/_{2}$-in [12-mm] cut and a 1-in [2.5-cm] cut. Skinny isn't always a good thing.

1 lb [455 g] sweet potatoes

2 pears

1 shallot

One 1-in [2.5-cm] knob fresh ginger

3 sprigs fresh thyme

1 Tbsp olive oil

Kosher salt and freshly ground black pepper

4 pork chops, 1 in [2.5 cm] thick, rested at room temperature for 30 minutes

2 Tbsp apple jelly

1. Line a sheet pan with aluminum foil and place it in the oven. Preheat the oven to 425°F [220°C].

2. On a large cutting board, peel the potatoes and dice into 1-in [2.5-cm] pieces. Peel and core the pears and cut them in the same way; transfer the potatoes and pears to a large bowl. Chop the shallot, peel and mince the ginger, and add them to the bowl along with the thyme (don't worry; you're going to pull the stems out later), olive oil, $^{1}/_{2}$ tsp salt, and a few grinds of pepper, mixing it all together with your hands. Remove the sheet pan from the oven and arrange the vegetables evenly on the hot pan. Roast the vegetables for 15 minutes.

3. While the vegetables roast, sprinkle the pork chops with $^{1}/_{2}$ tsp salt and a few grinds of pepper on both sides. Make room for the pork on the sheet pan and return to the oven for another 15 minutes, or until the pork reaches 145°F [60°C] on an instant-read thermometer and the potatoes are tender. Discard the thyme stems.

4. Spread a layer of apple jelly on the chops. Switch the oven setting to broil, return the pan to the second-highest rack, and broil for 1 to 2 minutes to create a glaze. Rest the pork for at least 3 minutes to allow the juices to settle. Divide the vegetables and chops among heated plates and serve immediately.

It's that easy: Today's pork is lean and clean and the trick to making a juicy chop is simple: just don't overcook it. Cook pork chops to an internal temperature of 145°F [60°C]. The temperature will continue to climb as they rest for a nice rosy middle.

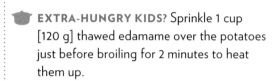 **EXTRA-HUNGRY KIDS?** Sprinkle 1 cup [120 g] thawed edamame over the potatoes just before broiling for 2 minutes to heat them up.

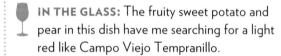 **ADULT TASTE BUDS?** Spread the adults' chops with Asian plum sauce instead of apple jelly for a more complex flavor.

IN THE GLASS: The fruity sweet potato and pear in this dish have me searching for a light red like Campo Viejo Tempranillo.

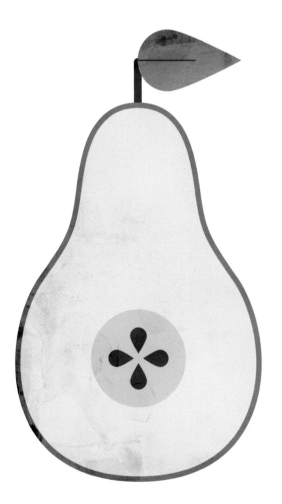

Rosemary Pork Tenderloin

with CARROTS and FIG-YOGURT SAUCE

Pork tenderloin has always been a favorite at our house because it's so good at partnering up with other flavors. Here, it's rubbed with woodsy rosemary, but fresh thyme or oregano would be just as good. Basic carrots and corn round out the meal, but the figs, fig-yogurt sauce, and pistachios take this dish to the next level with minimal effort.

7 dried Black Mission figs

¼ cup [35 g] pistachios

5 medium carrots, about 12 oz [340 g]

1 shallot

1 Tbsp olive oil, plus more for drizzling

Kosher salt and freshly ground black pepper

1½ lb [680 g] pork tenderloin

1 Tbsp chopped fresh rosemary

½ cup [120 g] plain Greek yogurt

¼ cup [75 g] fig jam

1 cup [140 g] frozen corn, thawed

1. Line a sheet pan with aluminum foil and place it in the oven. Preheat the oven to 425°F [220°C].

2. On a large cutting board, stem and quarter the figs; transfer them to a bowl and add hot tap water to cover.

3. Chop the pistachios and set aside. Peel and thinly slice the carrots and chop the shallot; transfer them to a medium bowl and toss them with the olive oil, a sprinkle of salt, and a few grinds of pepper.

4. On the cutting board, rub the pork with ½ tsp salt and a few grinds of pepper. Sprinkle the

rosemary over the pork and press so that it adheres. Drizzle with a little olive oil and pat it on with your fingers.

5. Arrange the pork on one side of the heated pan and the carrot mixture on the other side, spreading it out so that it cooks evenly. Roast the meat and vegetables for 20 minutes.

6. While the meat and vegetables cook, stir together the yogurt and jam and keep refrigerated.

continued

7. Check the meat for doneness with an instant-read thermometer. It should read 145°F [60°C]. Transfer the meat to a cutting board and tent with aluminum foil. Allow the meat to rest for at least 5 minutes to let the juices settle. Leave the thermometer in the meat while it rests and you will see the temperature rise to at least 150°F [65°C].

8. While the meat rests, drain the figs, toss them on top of the carrots, sprinkle the corn over the vegetables, and cook for another 5 minutes.

9. Slice the pork thinly and divide it and the vegetables among heated plates. Dollop with the yogurt sauce, sprinkle with the pistachios, and serve.

It's that easy: *Oddly, fig jam is often found in the cheese department at the grocery. I think many use it as a garnish for cheese plates and it's great served that way, but it's extra special dolloped onto a slice of grilled chicken or pork, elevating a basic meal to simply elegant.*

EXTRA-HUNGRY KIDS? Add extra carrots and corn.

ADULT TASTE BUDS? Cook up quartered baby bok choy with the carrots to balance some of the sweetness.

IN THE GLASS: Rosé is perfect with pork. Look for Whispering Angel. Yes, the angels do whisper about this wine. It's heavenly. And for heaven's sake, pour the kids a Shirley Temple.

Italian Sausage

with CABBAGE *and* LENTILS

Lentils are one of my secret weapons in the war to get dinner on the table. Earthy and meaty, they fill hungry tummies and adapt to endless flavorings and add-ins. I've gone the Italian route here with spicy sausage, Italian herbs, and cabbage (another of my tried-and-true basics) to make what might be the perfect one-pan meal. Packed with protein and fresh veggies, this dish proves how good simple can taste.

1 onion	*1 Tbsp olive oil*
3 garlic cloves	*1 lb [455 g] Italian sausage links (mild or spicy)*
1 carrot	*1 tsp Italian seasoning, plus more if needed*
½ head cabbage	*Kosher salt and freshly ground black pepper*
1½ cups [360 ml] beef or chicken broth	*1¼ cups [250 g] green or brown lentils, rinsed and picked over to remove stones*
¼ cup [60 ml] white wine or apple juice	
1 Tbsp cider vinegar, plus more if needed	*2 Tbsp minced fresh flat-leaf parsley*

1. On a large cutting board, chop the onion and garlic and peel and thinly slice the carrot. Transfer them to a medium bowl. Thinly slice the cabbage.

2. Combine the broth, wine, and vinegar in a measuring cup.

3. Heat a 12-in [30.5-cm] skillet over medium-high heat and add the olive oil. When the oil shimmers, add the sausages and brown them on all sides, about 6 minutes. Transfer the sausages to a plate. They won't be cooked through at this point.

4. Add the onion mixture, Italian seasoning, ½ tsp salt, and a few grinds of pepper to the pan and sauté until the vegetables begin to soften, about 3 minutes. Add the cabbage in batches, adding more as it turns bright green and wilts. Stir in the broth mixture and the lentils, pressing them down to submerge them, and bring to a simmer. Reduce the heat to low and simmer the mixture for 15 minutes, then nestle the sausages back into the pan and cook until the lentils are tender and the sausages

continued

are cooked through, about 10 minutes. Taste and add more salt, pepper, vinegar, or Italian seasoning if it needs it.

5. Divide the sausages and lentils among heated plates, sprinkle with parsley, and serve hot.

It's that easy: Lentils are a small but nutritionally mighty member of the legume family. They're a great source of fiber, which helps lower cholesterol, but they also help manage blood sugar levels, and they provide seven important minerals with virtually zero fat. Bring on the lentils!

EXTRA-HUNGRY KIDS? This brown meal could use a bit of green. Trim and slice broccoli stalks lengthwise 1/4 in [6 mm] thick and lay them in the pan on top of the sausages for the last 10 minutes of cooking.

ADULT TASTE BUDS? A salad of thinly sliced fennel and sliced oranges with a splash of lemon juice and a glug of olive oil adds a fresh note to this earthy meal.

IN THE GLASS: When in doubt, I say Beaujolais! I like mine a little colder than the usual glass of red. Try swirling an ice cube in the wine for a few seconds and then scoop it out to chill the wine but not water it down.

Sausage and Pepper Hoagies

with RED SAUCE

My bestie Suzy and I attend an annual antique show at a fairground in rural Ohio. We wake up at the crack of dawn, the better to grab the best platters, bowls, and bracelets before the general admission fans arrive. We make one pass around the track and then buy a sausage hoagie (because we deserve it) with onions and peppers for breakfast. It is the best thing in the world. But you don't have to wake up in the dark to enjoy these sausage hoagies. They're so easy, I feel a little guilty including them in the book, but what is so bad about remembering how good something so simple can be? Besides, maybe you never went to a fairground in the middle of summer and had one of these deliciously messy sandwiches. Breakfast or dinner, they are always a good thing.

2 onions	*4 to 6 hoagie buns, split*
1 green bell pepper	*1 Tbsp olive oil*
1 red or yellow bell pepper	*4 to 6 large Italian sausage links (mild or spicy)*
2 garlic cloves	*1 tsp Italian seasoning or herb mix*
1 cup [240 ml] jarred marinara sauce	*Kosher salt and freshly ground black pepper*
¼ cup [60 ml] white wine	*½ cup [40 g] shredded mozzarella cheese*

1. On a large cutting board, thinly slice the onions and bell peppers and mince the garlic. Combine the marinara and wine in a measuring cup.

2. Open the buns and pick some of the bread from the center to make a trough. (This allows you to fill the buns with more good stuff.) Set aside.

3. Heat a 12-in [30.5-cm] skillet over medium-high heat and add the olive oil. When the oil shimmers, add the sausages and brown them on all sides, about 6 minutes. Transfer them to a plate and keep warm. They won't be cooked through at this point.

4. Add the onions, bell peppers, Italian seasoning, a sprinkle of salt, and a few grinds of pepper to the pan and cook until the vegetables are softened, about 5 minutes. Add the garlic and cook another minute, or until fragrant. Pour in the marinara mixture and nestle the sausages into the sauce. Bring to a boil, cover, and reduce the heat to low. Simmer the sausages in the sauce until the sausages are cooked through and the peppers are tender, about 10 minutes.

5. While the sausages simmer, preheat the broiler, open up the buns, and toast them on the second-highest rack until warm and lightly browned, about 1 minute (watch closely or they'll burn).

6. Lay the buns on plates, fill them with the hot sausages, onions, and peppers, and top with the mozzarella. Serve.

It's that easy: If you don't want so much bread, try using Vienna rolls instead of the longer, thicker hoagie buns. Picking some of the bread out of the middle of the bun allows you to stuff more of the good stuff inside so it doesn't slide out every time you take a bite.

EXTRA-HUNGRY KIDS? Serve with salty potato chips or cook up a batch of frozen french fries.

ADULT TASTE BUDS? A salad would round out this meal's carby nature. Toss together butter lettuce, halved grape tomatoes, a splash of sherry vinegar, and a glug of olive oil, and season with salt and pepper.

IN THE GLASS: A cold beer makes this meal a celebration. Miller Light is in my fridge. What's in yours? Serve the kids a citrusy alcohol-free sangria of orange juice and cranberry juice with sliced lemon and orange. Don't forget a fun straw.

Italian Sausage

with GRAPE TOMATOES and POLENTA

If you've ever wondered what people do with those logs of polenta on the grocery shelf next to cornmeal, this is it. Making polenta from scratch is very easy, but it can take 30 minutes to cook, which is a little more time than I want to spend on a weeknight. So here, precooked polenta comes to the rescue with a quick sauté of spicy Italian sausage and sweet tomatoes and dinner is done. I love this dish for its simplicity, but mostly for the fact that this meal slides down into your tummy like a warm hug.

One 1-lb [455-g] log prepared polenta

1 onion

1 garlic clove

1 lb [455 g] spicy Italian sausage links

2 Tbsp olive oil, plus more if needed

10 oz [280 g] grape tomatoes

⅓ cup [80 ml] white wine, apple juice, or chicken broth

Kosher salt and freshly ground black pepper

6 oz [170 g] fresh mozzarella cheese

¼ cup [20 g] grated Parmesan cheese

¼ cup [10 g] fresh basil leaves

1. Preheat the oven to 375°F [190°C].

2. On a large cutting board, cut eight ½-in [2.5-cm] thick rounds from the log of polenta; transfer them to a plate. (Wrap the remaining polenta in plastic wrap and refrigerate for up to 1 week.)

3. Slice the onion and mince the garlic in separate piles. Cut the sausages into bite-size pieces.

4. Heat a 12-in [30.5-cm] ovenproof skillet over medium-high heat and add 1 Tbsp of the olive oil. When the oil shimmers, add the onion and sausage and sauté until the onion is soft and the sausage is

starting to brown, about 5 minutes. Add the garlic, tomatoes, and wine and continue to cook until the tomatoes begin to soften and heat up but are still whole, about 4 minutes. Sprinkle with salt and a few grinds of pepper; transfer the mixture to a large bowl and keep warm.

5. Add the remaining 1 Tbsp olive oil to the pan; when the oil shimmers, add half the polenta rounds and sprinkle them with salt and a few grinds of pepper. Cook until they are crispy on the bottom, about 2 minutes, then flip over and cook another 2 minutes to crisp up the other side. Transfer the rounds to a plate and keep warm while cooking the remaining rounds. You may have to add more oil.

6. Arrange the rounds in the bottom of the pan, overlapping if necessary, and top with the sausage-tomato mixture. Cut the mozzarella into thin slices and arrange evenly over the top, sprinkle with the Parmesan, and pop in the oven for 15 minutes to heat and melt the cheese.

7. Divide the polenta casserole among heated plates. Tear the basil into small pieces and sprinkle over the plates. Serve hot.

It's that easy: You won't use the whole log of polenta for this dish but here's a tip. Some night when you crave something hot and comforting, cut the remaining log into dice and cook it up with a cup or so of chicken broth. It will turn into a thick porridge. Stir in butter and serve with sautéed vegetables.

EXTRA-HUNGRY KIDS? A green salad is a nice addition. Toss baby greens, grated carrot, and cucumber with a splash of balsamic vinegar and a glug of olive oil.

ADULT TASTE BUDS? Add a bitter salad of thinly sliced radicchio, olives, sliced orange, a splash of white balsamic, and a glug of olive oil.

IN THE GLASS: A Tempranillo from Spain sounds just right. Fruity and lush, a bottling from Torremorón is spot-on.

Butter Bean Stew

with KIELBASA

I've been making a version of this stew for about thirty years. The one constant is the butter beans; they're creamy and luscious and so easy to just drain and toss in. The kielbasa is not only delicious in and of itself but it also adds a savory element to the stew, its garlicky essence permeating the broth. I love the fresh vegetables in this stew, but if you don't have them in the fridge, feel free to compose your own with whatever you have canned or in the freezer. Just think about color and texture and make it your own.

1 onion	*1 tsp dried oregano or basil or a mix of the two*
1 garlic clove	*4 cups [960 ml] beef broth*
2 carrots	*One 15-oz [425-g] can diced tomatoes with juice*
1 celery stalk	*Two 15-oz [425-g] cans butter beans, drained and rinsed*
1 zucchini	
1 lb [455 g] beef kielbasa	*2 Tbsp chopped fresh flat-leaf parsley*
1 Tbsp olive oil	*¼ cup [20 g] grated Parmesan cheese*

1. On a large cutting board, chop the onion and mince the garlic; transfer them to a small bowl. Peel and thinly slice the carrots and celery, then quarter the zucchini lengthwise and thinly slice it. Transfer the vegetables to a large bowl. Slice the kielbasa into bite-size pieces.

2. Heat a 4-qt [3.8-L] saucepan over medium-high heat and add the olive oil. When the oil shimmers, add the onion mixture and oregano and sauté until it begins to soften, about 2 minutes. Add the kielbasa and cook until the meat begins to crinkle around

the edges, about 2 minutes. Add the carrot mixture and continue to cook for another minute or so. You just want the vegetables to heat up a little bit.

3. Stir in the broth, tomatoes, and beans and bring to a boil. Reduce the heat to low and simmer for about 20 minutes, or until all the vegetables are tender and the flavors have blended. Stir in the parsley.

4. Ladle the hot stew into heated bowls and sprinkle with the Parmesan. Serve.

It's that easy: Pantry staples are at the heart of this stew, so make it a point to always have canned beans and tomatoes and boxed broth in your house. Even if you didn't have the vegetables there's a good chance you would have an assortment in the freezer, so you could make a vegetarian version of this stew without going to the grocery. Yes, you could.

 **EXTRA-HUNGRY KIDS?** Make grilled cheese sandwiches for dipping.

 **ADULT TASTE BUDS?** Add a sprinkle of paprika or smoked salt.

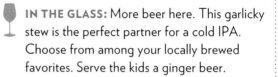 **IN THE GLASS:** More beer here. This garlicky stew is the perfect partner for a cold IPA. Choose from among your locally brewed favorites. Serve the kids a ginger beer.

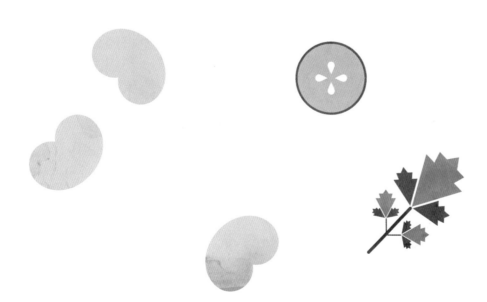

Kielbasa

with SAUERKRAUT, APPLE, and VEGETABLES

Every now and then I get a serious hankering for sauerkraut and kielbasa. There's something about the way the fatty, garlicky meat flavors the tart cabbage, each one benefiting from the attributes of the other. I like to spice it up with a hint of clove, bay, and allspice and then give it a simmer in white wine and chicken broth. It's less tart than many kraut dishes (which pleases the kids) and adults like some Dijon mustard on the side to slather over the meat and potatoes.

1 onion	*3/4 cup [180 ml] chicken broth*
1 carrot	*4 whole cloves*
1 tart-sweet apple, such as Braeburn or Crispin	*4 whole allspice berries*
6 new potatoes	*2 bay leaves*
1 lb [455 g] kielbasa, knockwurst, bratwurst, or a combination	*Kosher salt and freshly ground black pepper*
	2 lb [910 g] sauerkraut
8 oz [230 g] Canadian bacon	*1 Tbsp olive oil*
1 cup [240 ml] dry white wine	*1/4 cup [10 g] chopped flat-leaf parsley*

1. On a large cutting board, thinly slice the onion; transfer it to a bowl. Peel and slice the carrot, chop the apple, and slice the potatoes (do not peel); as you work, add them to the bowl. Slice the kielbasa into 2-in [5-cm] pieces, chop the bacon, and set aside. Combine the wine, broth, cloves, allspice, bay leaves, and 1 tsp salt in a large measuring cup. Drain and squeeze most of the juice from the sauerkraut.

2. Heat a 12-in [30.5-cm] skillet with a lid over medium-high heat and add the olive oil. When the oil shimmers, add the onion mixture and sauté until the onion is softened, about 3 minutes. Add the kielbasa, bacon, spiced broth mixture, sauerkraut, and a few grinds of pepper and stir it all together. Bring it to a simmer, cover, and reduce the heat to low. Simmer until the flavors have blended and the potatoes are tender, about 20 minutes. Pick out the cloves, allspice, and bay leaves.

3. Mound the sauerkraut and meat onto heated plates, sprinkle the parsley over the top, and serve.

ONE PAN, WHOLE FAMILY

It's that easy: *It's easy to vary this dish with an assortment of pork cuts. If you love bacon, fry some up at the beginning and use the fat to cook the vegetables. If you have the time for a longer cook (about 1 hour), add some diced salt pork for extra richness. I've added smoked pork chops and even a small pork butt to this basic recipe to great reviews, so by all means, play around with this one. It's very forgiving.*

EXTRA-HUNGRY KIDS? Add a few more ounces of meat, such as diced ham, smoked pork chops, or even hot dogs for those with less bold palates, and serve with a loaf of rye bread.

ADULT TASTE BUDS? Serve with grainy Dijon mustard and horseradish.

IN THE GLASS: When I eat a hot dog at the ballpark I want a beer to drink, and this meal makes me feel the same way. Beer is best, like a hoppy IPA, but if you insist on wine, go with a Riesling from Alsace, the classic French pairing. For the kids, pour cider from your local orchard.

Flat Iron Steak

with BROCCOLI SLAW

Slaw and steak are perfect dancing partners. The steak is rich and fatty and the slaw is tart and creamy. I like to have a little of each in every bite. Subbing in broccoli slaw for cabbage is easy and if you haven't tried its crunchy goodness, now is the time.

1½ lb [680 g] flat iron steak

Kosher salt and freshly ground black pepper

½ cup mayonnaise

2 Tbsp cider vinegar

1 Tbsp sugar

2 tsp Dijon mustard, plus more if needed

One 12-oz [340-g] bag broccoli slaw mix

⅓ cup [40 g] slivered almonds

1 Tbsp olive oil

1 lemon, cut into wedges

---

1. About 30 minutes before you plan to eat, transfer the steak from the fridge to the kitchen counter. This step removes the chill from the meat so that it cooks faster and more evenly, resulting in a juicier steak. Pat it dry with paper towels and season with salt and pepper on both sides.

2. While the steak rests, make the slaw. In a large bowl, stir together the mayonnaise, vinegar, sugar, mustard, ½ tsp salt, and a few grinds of pepper. Stir in the broccoli slaw and almonds and mix well. Taste and adjust the seasoning with more salt, pepper, or mustard if it needs it. Refrigerate the slaw if you're not using it right away.

3. Heat a 12-in [30.5-cm] skillet over medium-high heat and add the olive oil. When the oil shimmers, add the steak and cook until it has browned on that side, about 5 minutes. Try not to move it. It'll brown more quickly if you just let it do its business. Flip it over with tongs and cook for another 4 minutes for medium-rare meat or 5 minutes for medium. Reduce the heat if the bottom of the pan starts to burn or add a splash of water. Turn off the heat, remove the steak from the pan, and let it sit on a cutting board, tented with aluminum foil, for 3 or 4 minutes to let the juices settle before slicing. You could also grill the steak on a medium-high grill for 6 minutes on each side or until it registers 130°F [55°C] on an instant-read thermometer. The temperature will climb as it rests.

4. Slice the steak across the grain (look for fibrous lines that run through the steak and just cut crosswise on the diagonal) into thin slices and serve it on heated plates with a squeeze of lemon and a mound of broccoli slaw.

It's that easy: Inexpensive and surprisingly tender, the flat iron steak is from a tender part of the shoulder, so there's lots of marbling and flavor. Cook it like you would any steak, hot and fast, to medium-rare for best results.

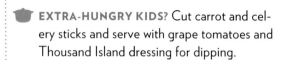

EXTRA-HUNGRY KIDS? Cut carrot and celery sticks and serve with grape tomatoes and Thousand Island dressing for dipping.

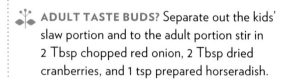

ADULT TASTE BUDS? Separate out the kids' slaw portion and to the adult portion stir in 2 Tbsp chopped red onion, 2 Tbsp dried cranberries, and 1 tsp prepared horseradish.

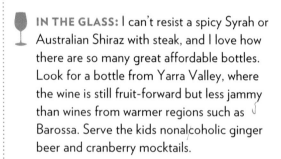

IN THE GLASS: I can't resist a spicy Syrah or Australian Shiraz with steak, and I love how there are so many great affordable bottles. Look for a bottle from Yarra Valley, where the wine is still fruit-forward but less jammy than wines from warmer regions such as Barossa. Serve the kids nonalcoholic ginger beer and cranberry mocktails.

Beef Kebabs

with ZUCCHINI and TOMATOES

What is it about meat on a stick? It's festive and fun and tastes absolutely fabulous! With the addition of a few vegetables, it becomes—tah-dah—a meal on a stick. Just fire up the grill and pop these kebabs over the flame for an easy-peasy dinner with almost zero cleanup.

1 large zucchini	*2 Tbsp olive oil*
1 lb [455 g] top sirloin	*1 Tbsp ras al hanout*
1 lime	*Kosher salt and freshly ground black pepper*
2 garlic cloves	*1 cup [240 g] store-bought hummus*
10 oz [275 g] cherry tomatoes	

1. Soak twelve flat 6-in [15-cm] wooden skewers (they hold the food more firmly than metal ones do) in a shallow dish filled with water for at least 10 minutes.

2. Preheat the grill to medium-high heat.

3. On a large cutting board, cut the zucchini and sirloin into 1-in [2.5-cm] cubes. Cut the lime in half and squeeze the juice into a medium bowl. Mince the garlic and add it to the bowl.

4. Add the sirloin, zucchini, tomatoes, olive oil, ras al hanout, 1 tsp salt, and a few grinds of pepper to the bowl and toss to coat.

5. Because the meat and vegetables cook at different rates, thread the meat and vegetables separately on the skewers. Sprinkle with salt and a few grinds of pepper.

6. Grill the skewers for 4 minutes, then turn and cook for another 3 minutes, or until the meat is medium (it should register 135°F to 140°F [57°C to 60°C] on an instant-read thermometer), and the vegetables are tender and browned. (If cooking in the oven, preheat the broiler. Arrange the skewers on a broiler pan on the second-highest rack and broil for 3 minutes on each side for medium meat.)

7. Serve the kebabs on individual plates on top of a dollop of hummus.

It's that easy: *Ras al hanout is a spice blend incorporating cinnamon, ginger, anise, nutmeg, cardamom, and cloves. I find myself sprinkling it over grilled chicken, fish, and beef, and vegetables as well. It is slightly sweet, so most kids like it. If you can't find it, use any spice blend you have in the pantry, such as Montreal Steak Seasoning.*

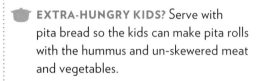 **EXTRA-HUNGRY KIDS?** Serve with pita bread so the kids can make pita rolls with the hummus and un-skewered meat and vegetables.

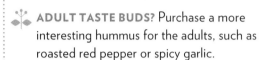 **ADULT TASTE BUDS?** Purchase a more interesting hummus for the adults, such as roasted red pepper or spicy garlic.

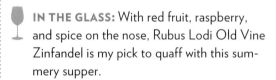 **IN THE GLASS:** With red fruit, raspberry, and spice on the nose, Rubus Lodi Old Vine Zinfandel is my pick to quaff with this summery supper.

Thai Steak Salad

I have a saying about Thai food, that it's like a party in your mouth. If that is the case, this Thai Steak Salad is the fireworks on New Year's Eve. In this iteration, green cilantro and mint, crunchy romaine, and a spicy/sweet lime dressing liven up simply broiled or grilled flank steak. You could add more ingredients to this salad, but it's pretty perfect just like this.

½ serrano or Thai chile

2 garlic cloves

½ cup [120 ml] fresh lime juice

3 Tbsp brown sugar

3 Tbsp vegetable oil

1 Tbsp fish sauce

Kosher salt and freshly ground black pepper

1 lb [455 g] flank or skirt steak, at room temperature

2 to 3 hearts romaine lettuce, depending on how much salad you want

½ cup [20 g] chopped fresh cilantro

½ cup [20 g] chopped fresh mint

½ small red onion, thinly sliced

10 oz [280 g] grape tomatoes, halved lengthwise

1. Preheat the grill or broiler to medium-high heat. If using a broiler, line a sheet pan with aluminum foil.

2. On a large cutting board, mince the chile (be careful touching the seeds and ribs, as they can be hot) and garlic; transfer to a medium bowl. Add the lime juice, sugar, 2 Tbsp of the vegetable oil, the fish sauce, and ¼ tsp salt. Stir to dissolve the sugar and set aside.

3. Sprinkle the steak with salt and a few grinds of pepper and drizzle it with the remaining 1 Tbsp vegetable oil.

4. Grill the steak for about 6 minutes on each side for medium-rare meat. If using an instant-read thermometer, look for a temperature of 130°F [55°C] because the temperature will climb as it rests. Thicker steaks may require longer cooking times. Transfer the steak to a cutting board and let it rest for at least 10 minutes to settle the juices before cutting. If using the broiler, place the steak on the prepared sheet pan and broil for 6 minutes, then turn and broil for another 5 minutes for medium-rare meat.

continued

5. While the steak is resting, chop the romaine, add to a large bowl, add the cilantro and mint, and toss it all together. Thinly slice the onion and halve the tomatoes and set them aside.

6. Divide the greens among dinner plates and scatter the onion and tomatoes over the top. Thinly slice the steak across the grain and divide the meat among the plates. Drizzle the dressing over the steak and greens and serve immediately.

It's that easy: There is a constant conundrum about heat when cooking with fresh chiles. The question is usually how hot is the chile and the answer is you don't know until you taste it. I have the habit of cutting off the tip of the chile and touching it to my tongue a few times until I either feel a burn or don't. One pepper in the bunch might be as hot as Hades and the rest might be mild or vice versa. In any case, always check before chucking a whole pepper in a recipe and remember your audience; you can always serve the kids first and then add the hot pepper to the adults' portions.

EXTRA-HUNGRY KIDS? Cook up some ramen noodles to serve under the greens. They soak up the dressing in a really nice way.

ADULT TASTE BUDS? You can always gild the lily by adding chopped peanuts, mango, basil, grated carrot, and green onions to amp up the party factor.

IN THE GLASS: A Riesling from Poet's Leap has the perfect tart and sweet notes to go with this tart and sweet salad.

Beef Fajitas

with GUACAMOLE

The control freak in me loves fajitas. I get to make each flavorful bite exactly the way I like it. I'm a fan of lots of vegetables, a little meat, and lots of guacamole, but my husband likes lots of cheese and meat, less vegetables, but still lots of guac. How do you like yours?

1½ lb [680 g] London broil	1 poblano chile or green bell pepper
2 garlic cloves	2 ripe avocados
4 limes	2 Tbsp chopped fresh cilantro
2 Tbsp vegetable oil	Eight to twelve 6-in [15-cm] flour tortillas
1 tsp ground cumin	Crumbled queso fresco
Kosher salt and freshly ground black pepper	Sour cream
1 small red onion	Jarred or fresh salsa
1 red bell pepper	

1. On a large cutting board, cut the steak into thin strips and then into bite-size pieces. Transfer the steak to a zippered plastic bag.

2. Flip the cutting board over onto the clean side, mince the garlic and add half to the steak. Juice three of the limes and add two-thirds of the juice to the steak along with 1 Tbsp of the vegetable oil, the cumin, ½ tsp salt, and a few grinds of pepper. Mush the marinade around, squeeze out the extra air, zip the bag closed, and let it rest on the counter while you prepare the other ingredients. (I like marinating the steak in the bag because the marinade really covers the surface of the meat, but if you'd rather

just place it all in a casserole or shallow dish, that is fine as well.)

3. Thinly slice the onion and then mince about 2 Tbsp of it; place the minced onion in a medium bowl and the sliced onion in a larger bowl. Seed and thinly slice the bell pepper and poblano and transfer them to the bowl with the sliced onion.

4. Halve and pit the avocados, then, using a large spoon, scoop the avocado flesh into the bowl with the minced onion and add the cilantro. Mash it all together with the back of a fork. Add the remaining

continued

LET'S EAT MEAT

one-third lime juice, a sprinkle of salt, and a few grinds of pepper. Taste and add more salt, pepper, or lime juice if it needs it and set the guacamole aside.

5. Heat a 12-in [30.5-cm] skillet over medium-high heat and add the remaining 1 Tbsp vegetable oil. When the oil shimmers, add the sliced onion and peppers and the remaining half of the garlic. Sprinkle the vegetables with 1/2 tsp salt and a few grinds of pepper and sauté them until they're tender but still a little crisp, about 5 minutes. Transfer the veggies to a large platter.

6. Add the meat and marinade to the hot pan and sprinkle the meat with salt and a few grinds of pepper. Sauté the meat, stirring every now and then, until medium-rare, about 2 minutes. Transfer the meat to the platter with the vegetables. There should be marinade remaining in the pan. Continue to cook for another minute until it reduces somewhat, and then pour it over the meat and vegetables.

7. Warm the tortillas on a plate, covered with microwave-safe plastic wrap, in the microwave for 30 seconds to 1 minute. Slice the remaining lime into wedges.

8. Lay out the platter of meat and vegetables, warm tortillas, guacamole, cheese, sour cream, lime wedges, and salsa on the table and make your own personal fajitas just the way you like them.

It's that easy: *It isn't easy to cook a whole steak to the perfect doneness. I can tell you how to do it, but it's the weeknight and you're tired and I'm tired and there is a better way to cook steak for fajitas on family night: cut it into small pieces so that the marinade flavors it more fully and it cooks more quickly and efficiently.*

EXTRA-HUNGRY KIDS? Open a can of refried beans and warm them up in the microwave. Serve them with the fajita fixings and either load the beans onto your fajita or serve them alongside.

ADULT TASTE BUDS? Add pickled jalapeños, chopped lettuce, and Mexican hot sauce to the spread.

IN THE GLASS: Fajitas and beer just go together. Drink your favorite. Mine is a Corona Light longneck with a slice of lime, but any brew will do. Serve the kids an Arnold Palmer: half iced tea, half lemonade.

OPEN-FACED

Super Burgers

with CHEDDAR, MUSHROOMS, and ONION

Every family needs a good burger in the dinner repertoire, and this is ours. For the record, I'm over trying to make tender, juicy burgers from lean ground beef. They end up like hockey pucks every time. So I just use a grind of beef that's 85 percent lean and toss in a few slices of finely chopped smoky bacon and a little olive oil as well. When served with mushrooms and onions, these burger bombs are almost as good as a rib-eye steak for a fraction of the cost.

1 onion	*3 Tbsp olive oil*
8 oz [230 g] cremini or button mushrooms	*1 Tbsp all-purpose flour*
1 garlic clove	*½ cup [120 ml] beef broth*
2 slices bacon	*¾ cup [60 g] grated Cheddar cheese*
1 lb [455 g] 85 percent lean ground beef	*4 slices sourdough bread*
1 Tbsp Worcestershire sauce	*Your favorite condiments, such as ketchup, mustard, and mayonnaise*
1 tsp steak and burger seasoning, plus more for sprinkling	*Pickles*
Kosher salt and freshly ground black pepper	*Sliced tomato*

1. On a large cutting board, slice the onion and mushrooms and mince the garlic. Transfer it all to a medium bowl. Chop the bacon as finely as you can (see "It's that easy"). In a large bowl, combine the bacon, beef, Worcestershire, steak and burger seasoning, ½ tsp salt, a few grinds of pepper, and 1 Tbsp of the olive oil. Mix gently with your hands just until combined and gently shape into four patties about 4 in [10 cm] in diameter.

2. Heat a 12-in [30.5-cm] skillet over medium-high heat and add 1 Tbsp of the olive oil. When the oil shimmers, add the burgers and cook until browned on the bottom, about 3 minutes. Flip them over and cook for another 3 minutes for medium burgers or 4 minutes for medium-well. Transfer the burgers to a plate and keep warm.

3. Add the remaining 1 Tbsp olive oil and the onion mixture to the pan along with a sprinkle of salt and a few grinds of pepper. Sauté, stirring every now and then, until the onion is tender and the mushrooms have browned, about 5 minutes. Stir in the flour and cook for another minute, stirring. Add the broth and stir until slightly thickened, about 1 minute. Reduce the heat to low, return the patties to the pan, and spoon the mushrooms and sauce over them. Top with the grated cheese. Cover and cook until the cheese melts, about 2 minutes.

4. Toast the bread in a toaster. Spread the toasted bread with the accompaniments of your choice and top with the burgers and mushrooms. Serve hot.

It's that easy: *It's so much easier to chop bacon if you take the time to place it on a plate in your freezer for about 10 minutes or so, until it's partially frozen, then finely dice it.*

EXTRA-HUNGRY KIDS? Toss some frozen fries or tater tots on a sheet pan and crisp them up in the oven while the burgers cook.

ADULT TASTE BUDS? Add more interesting cheese to the adult portions. Pepper Jack or Jarlsberg, anyone?

IN THE GLASS: I like Zinfandel with burgers. Maybe it's the combination of sweet ketchup, mayo, and tangy pickles inside the bun, but an old vine Zin from Lodi pairs really well with this recipe.

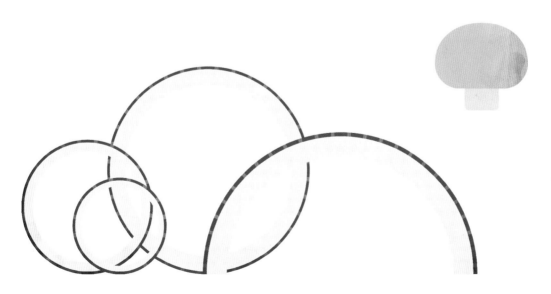

BARBECUE
Meat Loaf Patties
with HERBED SMASHED POTATOES *and* GREEN BEANS

If you grew up loving a dinner of meat loaf and mashed potatoes, you're going to love the ease and speed of this weeknight favorite. The meat loaf mixing process is simplified by using ground beef and sausage instead of a giant package of meat loaf mix, and the loaf patties are paired up with smashed new potatoes topped with sour cream and chives instead of whipped potatoes. I actually love the crispy bottoms and fluffy insides of these little roasted potatoes and definitely prefer not to pull out the mixer on a weeknight.

12 small new potatoes	8 oz [230 g] bulk Italian sausage
2 Tbsp olive oil	1 egg
Kosher salt and freshly ground black pepper	6 Tbsp barbecue sauce, plus more if desired
1 carrot	3 cups [570 g] frozen green beans, thawed
½ cup [30 g] panko bread crumbs	⅔ cup [160 g] sour cream
¼ cup [60 ml] milk	2 Tbsp minced fresh chives
1 lb [455 g] 85 percent lean ground beef	

1. Line a sheet pan with aluminum foil and place it in the oven. Preheat the oven to 425°F [220°C].

2. On a large cutting board, cut the potatoes in half (do not peel); transfer them to a medium bowl. Toss with the olive oil, ½ tsp salt, and a few grinds of pepper. Peel and grate the carrot into a pile.

3. In a large bowl, combine the panko and milk and allow the milk to be absorbed, about 1 minute. Add the carrot, beef, sausage, egg, ½ tsp salt, and a few grinds of pepper and mix with your hands

just until combined (overworking the mixture can make the meat loaf tough). Shape into six 4-in [10-cm] patties.

4. Remove the hot sheet pan from the oven and arrange the patties on one side and the potatoes skin side down on the other side. Return to the oven and roast for 20 minutes.

5. Top each patty with 1 Tbsp barbecue sauce, scatter the green beans over the open spaces, and return to the oven until the patties register 160°F [70°C] on an instant-read thermometer and the potatoes and beans are tender, about 5 minutes. If the potatoes are large and not quite soft enough, remove the patties to a plate and keep warm and roast the potatoes for another 5 minutes.

6. Smash the potatoes with the back of a fork and top each with a little extra salt, a dollop of sour cream, and a sprinkle of chives. Transfer the potatoes, beans, and meat loaf patties to heated plates. Serve hot with extra barbecue sauce if desired.

It's that easy: *The grated carrot in the meat loaf adds moisture and nutrition, so don't skip this step. If you don't have a carrot, a parsnip would work just as well.*

EXTRA-HUNGRY KIDS? A light green salad is a traditional accompaniment. Toss together spring mix greens with extra grated carrot, sliced cucumber, a splash of balsamic vinegar, and a glug of olive oil.

ADULT TASTE BUDS? Top the adults' potatoes with a combination of blue cheese, sour cream, ranch dressing, and Sriracha.

IN THE GLASS: If you're searching for a versatile wine that goes with all kinds of casual food, look for a bottle of Kermit Lynch Côtes du Rhône, a great weeknight-priced bottle.

Cowboy Chili

with CORN BREAD CRUST

I'd be lying if I didn't admit to feeding my clan this one-pot wonder for the past twenty years. It's full of meat and beans and the corn bread topping picks up loads of chili flavor as it cooks on top. Only you know how spicy your family likes their chili, so scale back on the chili powder if you have sensitive palates, but we like it just the way it is.

1 onion

1 red bell pepper

1 poblano chile or green bell pepper

1/4 cup [10 g] fresh cilantro

2 garlic cloves

3 Tbsp chili powder

Kosher salt and freshly ground black pepper

1 Tbsp olive oil

1 lb [455 g] 85 percent lean ground beef

One 15-oz [425-g] can kidney beans, drained and rinsed

One 8-oz [227-g] can tomato sauce

1/2 cup [70 g] frozen corn

1 cup [80 g] grated Cheddar cheese

Corn Bread Topping

1/2 cup [70 g] all-purpose flour

1/2 cup [70 g] cornmeal

1 Tbsp sugar

1 tsp baking powder

1/2 tsp kosher salt

1 egg

1/2 cup [120 ml] milk

2 Tbsp vegetable oil

1. On a large cutting board, chop the onion, bell pepper, poblano chile, cilantro, and garlic. Transfer it all to a large bowl. In a small bowl, combine the chili powder, 1 1/2 tsp salt, and a few grinds of pepper.

2. Heat a 12-in [30.5-cm] skillet over medium-high heat and add the olive oil. When the oil shimmers, add the chopped vegetable mixture and chili powder mixture to the pan. Sauté the vegetables, stirring every now and then, until the vegetables begin to soften, about 4 minutes.

continued

3. Crumble the ground beef into the skillet and cook the meat, breaking it up with a spatula, until no longer pink, about 4 minutes. Add the beans, tomato sauce, corn, and 1/3 cup [80 ml] water and bring to a boil. Cover, reduce the heat to medium-low or low, and simmer for 10 minutes.

4. For the corn bread topping: While the chili cooks, in a medium bowl, combine the flour, cornmeal, sugar, baking powder, and salt. In another small bowl, beat the egg and stir in the milk and vegetable oil. Stir the liquid into the dry ingredients, just until blended.

5. Sprinkle the cheese over the top of the chili and pour the corn bread batter evenly over the top, smoothing with the back of a spatula to make it an even thickness. Cover and continue to cook until the corn bread is firm and cooked through, about 10 minutes.

6. Scoop the chili and corn bread into heated shallow bowls and dig in.

It's that easy: If you are just too overwhelmed to make the corn bread topping, omit that step and go ahead and set a purchased corn bread on the table for an easy fix.

EXTRA-HUNGRY KIDS? Add an extra 1/2 cup [70g] of corn. It will also make the chili a little sweeter, which isn't a bad thing to tempt the little ones.

ADULT TASTE BUDS? Add a garnish of thinly sliced green onion, sour cream, and pickled jalapeños to the adult portions.

IN THE GLASS: It can be difficult to match up chili with wine, but just about any beer, from Pabst Blue Ribbon to your local brew, will work very nicely. Serve the kids a blend of pineapple juice, orange juice, and club soda.

Beef Paprikash

with SWEET POTATOES and NOODLES

Beef paprikash is one of the homiest dishes you'll find. The antidote to a rough day, a hot bowl of paprikash topped with sour cream is meant to be savored slowly with those you love. This version is rich with sweet potatoes, steak, paprika, and egg noodles—exactly what the doctor ordered on a cold, dark night.

1 lb [455 g] sweet potatoes	*2 Tbsp tomato paste*
1 lb [455 g] top sirloin or flat iron steak	*1 Tbsp paprika*
Kosher salt and freshly ground black pepper	*4 cups [960 ml] beef broth*
1 onion	*4 oz [115 g] egg noodles*
1 celery stalk	*2 Tbsp red wine vinegar*
1 garlic clove	*¼ cup [60 g] sour cream*
1 Tbsp olive oil	*2 Tbsp chopped fresh parsley*

1. On a large cutting board, peel the potatoes and dice into 1-in [2.5-cm] pieces; transfer them to a medium bowl. Cut the steak into bite-size pieces, transfer it to a medium bowl, and sprinkle with ½ tsp salt and a few grinds of pepper. Flip the board over to the clean side and chop the onion, thinly slice the celery, and mince the garlic into a pile.

2. Heat a 4-qt [3.8-L] saucepan over medium-high heat and add the olive oil. When the oil shimmers, add half the meat and brown it, without moving it, for about 3 minutes. Stir in the remaining meat, the onion, celery, garlic, tomato paste, paprika, and ½ tsp salt and continue to cook until the vegetables begin to soften, 2 to 3 minutes. Add the broth and potatoes and stir up all the browned bits on the bottom of the pan. Bring to a boil, reduce the heat to low, and simmer, uncovered, until the potatoes are almost tender, about 10 minutes. Raise the heat to medium, stir in the noodles, and cook until tender, about 5 minutes. Careful not to let it bubble too fast. You don't want the liquid to reduce too much.

3. Stir in the vinegar and taste for seasoning, adding salt and pepper if it needs it.

continued

LET'S EAT MEAT

4. Ladle the hot stew into heated bowls, add a dollop of sour cream, and sprinkle with the parsley. Serve.

It's that easy: *If this stew were cooked slowly, the traditional way, you could use a cheaper, tougher cut of meat. The more tender top sirloin or flat iron steak is used here because it doesn't need a long simmer to tenderize, allowing you to get dinner on the table much sooner.*

EXTRA-HUNGRY KIDS? Add five or six new potatoes, diced like the sweet potatoes, to bulk up the stew.

ADULT TASTE BUDS? Ladle the kids' portions, then add 1/2 cup [120 g] drained canned sauerkraut to the pot. Stir for a minute to reheat and serve. It adds a delicious tang!

IN THE GLASS: Look for a medium-bodied Côtes du Rhône to partner up with this homey stew. A Belgian ale wouldn't be a bad choice either.

Go Fish

Shrimp Pizza

with PINEAPPLE and SPINACH

I've been making pizza on Friday nights for as long as I can remember. It started out as a way to save money and ended up just being a tastier and healthier alternative to take-out. Plus, it's so nice to be able to tailor your pizza just the way you like it. In this pizza topper, tart pineapple and sweet grape tomatoes make a great partner with succulent shrimp, spinach, and Monterey Jack cheese. Try this fast and fresh option on pizza Friday and you'll be eating a delicious, fresh, and healthy pizza faster than you can order in. Maybe you should make two so you have plenty.

½ shallot

6 oz [170 g] grape tomatoes

12 oz [340 g] cooked, deveined, tail-off shrimp

1 lb [455 g] frozen pizza dough, thawed and out of the refrigerator for about 10 minutes

1 Tbsp olive oil

Kosher salt and freshly ground black pepper

1 cup [20 g] baby spinach

¼ cup [55 g] pineapple tidbits, drained

1½ cups [120 g] grated Monterey Jack cheese

1. If you have a pizza stone, place it on the bottom rack of the oven. If you don't have a stone, you can bake the pizza on a sheet pan. (It won't be as crispy on the bottom and may take a few more minutes to bake.) Preheat the oven to 450°F [230°C].

2. On a large cutting board, mince the shallot and halve the tomatoes. Cut the shrimp into bite-size pieces if they are large.

3. On a lightly floured surface, pat and stretch out the dough into a 16-in [40.5-cm] circle and place it on a sheet of parchment paper. Transfer the dough and parchment to a pizza peel or a sheet pan. Drizzle the dough with the olive oil, rub the shallot over the top with your fingers, and sprinkle with salt and a few grinds of pepper. Layer with the spinach, pineapple, tomatoes, and shrimp and top with the cheese.

4. Slide the pizza, still on the parchment, onto the heated pizza stone or transfer the sheet pan to the oven. Bake until the bottom is crispy and the cheese has browned slightly, 12 to 15 minutes.

5. Slide the peel under the pizza to remove it from the stone or transfer the sheet pan to a wire rack. Let the pizza cool for about 5 minutes before cutting into wedges. Serve hot.

It's that easy: *I like to think of pizza recipes as suggestions and encourage you to freestyle your own pies with an eye to your family's preferences. Try making this pizza with whole-wheat pizza dough and add some grated carrot with the pineapple. It adds a bit more nutrition and color and tastes even better.*

EXTRA-HUNGRY KIDS? Add some diced ham or Canadian bacon to the topping and this pizza becomes a classic.

ADULT TASTE BUDS? Turn to the Asian-Style Fish Tacos recipe (page 195). There's a recipe for pickled onions in the "It's that easy" tip that are delicious sprinkled over the adult portions of the pizza.

IN THE GLASS: Txakolina (chock-oh-lee-nah) or Txakoli (chock-oh-lee) is a spritzy, zippy, light-bodied white or rosé from the Basque Country in Spain and well worth the search. Lightly fizzy, Txakolina pairs beautifully with seafood, cheese, and this pizza, of course. It's pizza night, so serve the kids something sparkly as well, like a peach-mango juice blend lightened with sparkling water.

START TO FINISH
30 minutes
. . .
HANDS-ON TIME
25 minutes
. . .
SERVES
4

Red Curry Shrimp

A curry is just a glorified stir-fry. But oh, what a stir-fry. I've streamlined this curry with fewer ingredients but no less flavor: it's rich with coconut milk, colorful veggies, and juicy shrimp. This dish may seem exotic, but once you've purchased fish sauce and red curry paste, the remaining ingredients are all familiar. Most kids like curry if it isn't too spicy, so add the curry paste according your family's preferences. Remember that you can always add more but you can't take it out once it's in there.

1 onion	*1¹/₂ Tbsp brown sugar*
1 red bell pepper	*1¹/₂ Tbsp fish sauce*
1 garlic clove	*Kosher salt and freshly ground black pepper*
1¹/₂ lb [680 g] broccoli florets	*1 Tbsp vegetable oil*
2 limes	*1 lb [455 g] small shrimp, peeled and deveined*
One 14-oz [400-g] can unsweetened coconut milk	*Two 8- to 10-oz [227- to 283-g] bags frozen precooked rice*
¹/₂ cup [120 g] vegetable broth	*¹/₄ cup [10 g] minced fresh cilantro*
2 Tbsp Thai red curry paste, plus more if needed	

1. On a large cutting board, thinly slice the onion and bell pepper and mince the garlic. Transfer to a medium bowl. Cut the broccoli into bite-size pieces. Juice one lime into a small bowl and cut the other lime into wedges; set aside. Combine the coconut milk, broth, curry paste, sugar, fish sauce, and ¹/₂ tsp salt in another medium bowl or a large measuring cup.

2. Heat a 12-in [30.5-cm] skillet over medium-high heat and add the vegetable oil. When the oil shimmers, add the onion mixture and sauté the vegetables, stirring every now and then, until they begin to soften, about 2 minutes. Stir in the coconut milk mixture, bring it to a boil, then reduce the heat to low and cook, stirring every now and then, until it reduces and thickens, about 5 minutes. Stir in the broccoli and shrimp and increase the heat so that it comes to a boil. Reduce the heat again to low, cover, and cook gently until the shrimp are cooked through, the broccoli is tender, and the flavors have blended, about 5 minutes.

3. While the curry cooks, cook the rice according to the package directions.

4. Stir the lime juice and half the cilantro into the curry and fine-tune the taste by adding salt, pepper, or more red curry paste if it needs it.

5. Mound the hot rice into heated shallow bowls, ladle the curry over the rice, and sprinkle with the remaining cilantro. Serve with lime wedges on the side for more zing.

It's that easy: You can find curry pastes in the international section of many grocery stores either in small cans or jars or in larger cardboard containers. Store curry paste in the refrigerator after opening and it will keep for months and months. Or go ahead and freeze Tbsp-size blobs on a parchment-lined sheet pan and then transfer them to a zippered freezer bag to keep frozen for a year or so.

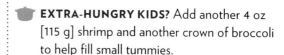 **EXTRA-HUNGRY KIDS?** Add another 4 oz [115 g] shrimp and another crown of broccoli to help fill small tummies.

 **ADULT TASTE BUDS?** Serve the kids' portions and then stir in another couple tsp of curry paste over medium heat until well blended. Top adult portions with chopped cashews and/or toasted coconut.

IN THE GLASS: When dinner is spicy, I like an off-dry Riesling. It has a little sugar, which tames the heat and doesn't compete with all the flavor on the plate. For a great weeknight bottle, look for Nein Lives Riesling from the Mosel region in Germany.

Bow Ties with Shrimp,

SPINACH, *and* FETA

I had a great time figuring out how to best cook this pasta dish in one pan. Turns out, cooking the pasta in a mixture of vegetable broth, water, and lemon juice flavors the pasta in the best possible way, and then there's all that shrimp, spinach, and feta cheese crumbled in, making it taste even more fabulous. The end result is lemony, cheesy pasta and shrimp for dinner, all in about 40 minutes.

1 onion	*1 lb [455 g] bow tie pasta*
2 garlic cloves	*1 lb [455 g] small to medium shrimp, shelled and deveined*
2 cups [480 ml] vegetable broth	
2 lemons	*8 oz [230 g] baby spinach*
1 Tbsp olive oil	*8 oz [230 g] feta cheese, crumbled*
	Kosher salt and freshly ground black pepper

1. On a large cutting board, chop the onion and mince the garlic in separate piles. Combine the vegetable broth and 1½ cups [360 ml] water in a large liquid measuring cup, then grate the zest from one of the lemons into the cup. Squeeze the juice from both lemons into the cup.

2. Heat a 12-in [30.5-cm] skillet over medium-high heat and add the olive oil. When the oil shimmers, add the onion and sauté until it begins to soften, about 2 minutes. Stir in the garlic and cook for another minute, or until fragrant.

3. Pour in the broth mixture and add the pasta, pressing down on the pasta to submerge it. Bring to

a boil, reduce the heat to medium-low, and simmer the pasta for about 10 minutes, uncovered, stirring every now and then. It shouldn't be completely tender yet. If the pasta isn't submerged, add another ½ cup [120 ml] water.

4. Stir in the shrimp and continue to cook, stirring, until the shrimp are almost cooked through, about 3 minutes. Stir in the spinach in batches, adding more as each previous bunch wilts, and then stir in the cheese. This will take a few minutes and the pasta and shrimp will have a chance to tenderize.

continued

There should be a little sauce in the bottom of the pan. If not, stir in another 1/4 cup [60 ml] water to juice it up. Taste and season with salt and pepper if it needs it.

5. Heap the pasta onto heated plates and serve immediately. It's best when really hot.

It's that easy: *Bagged frozen shrimp come in a variety of sizes. The numbers 41/50 on the label indicate that there are 41 to 50 shrimp in 1 lb [455 g]; these are usually considered medium. Small shrimp are labeled 51/60 and those labeled 36/40 are considered medium-large. I suggest the small to medium shrimp for pasta or mixed seafood dishes. But if your shrimp are on the large side, cut them down into smaller pieces so you get more bites of pasta with shrimp in them.*

EXTRA-HUNGRY KIDS? It's not likely, as this makes a ton of pasta, but if you're looking for a little extra, just add another 4 oz [115 g] shrimp.

ADULT TASTE BUDS? I like my serving with a generous sprinkle of red pepper flakes and an extra squeeze of lemon juice.

IN THE GLASS: Tart feta cheese is challenging but my favorite pairing with this dish (and a general fave overall) is a zippy white like a Sauvignon Blanc from New Zealand. For the kids, pour a blend of pineapple juice and coconut water and add an orange slice to the glass.

Snapper Papillote

with SUMMER VEGETABLES and HERB BUTTER

En papillote is a fancy French term for cooking in a bag or package. Parchment is the traditional packaging, but foil is so much easier to work with on a weeknight. I fell in love with this simple technique in cooking school thirty years ago and truth be told, it's the same technique we used at Girl Scout camp when we made campfire hobo dinners with hot dogs and canned vegetables. Because you are cooking fresh vegetables, cut them small so they cook fast and make sure the package has a tight seal so that everything comes out of the hot oven tender and juicy from the steamy environment. You can easily cook these packages on the grill over medium-high heat. In about 15 minutes, dinner is done.

2 zucchini	*1 lemon*
1 orange or yellow bell pepper	*3 Tbsp basil pesto, store-bought or homemade*
8 oz [224 g] grape tomatoes	*Kosher salt and freshly ground black pepper*
½ shallot	*3 Tbsp unsalted butter, softened*
2 garlic cloves	*Four 6-oz [170-g] red snapper fillets*

1. Place a sheet pan in the oven and preheat the oven to 425°F [220°C].

2. On a large cutting board, halve and thinly slice the zucchini. Thinly slice the bell pepper, halve the tomatoes, chop the shallot, and mince the garlic. As you work, transfer the vegetables to a large bowl. Zest and juice the lemon separately and sprinkle half the zest and half the juice over the vegetables. Add 2 Tbsp of the pesto, ½ tsp salt, and a few grinds of pepper and toss to combine. In a small bowl, combine the remaining 1 Tbsp pesto with the butter and remaining zest and lemon juice and set it aside.

3. Sprinkle the snapper with salt and a few grinds of pepper.

4. Cut four sheets of aluminum foil about 15 in [38 cm] wide and lay them out on a work surface. Fold them in half to make a crease, then open them back up again.

continued

5. Divide the vegetables among the foil sheets, placing them on one side close to the folded edge and spreading them out so that they cook evenly. Top with the fish and spoon a dollop of the butter mixture onto each fillet.

6. Fold the foil back over the fish and vegetables and roll the edge to make a good seal.

7. Remove the sheet pan from the oven and arrange the foil packets on the hot pan. Bake until the vegetables are tender, about 20 minutes.

8. Using a wide spatula, transfer the packets (there's juice in there) to heated plates and carefully open them (hot steam may escape) at the table. Serve hot.

It's that easy: *Any fish can work in this recipe, so buy whatever is freshest. Ask the fishmonger which fish in the case came in that day, as most stores receive shipments daily. I've made this dish with halibut, salmon, haddock, tilapia, and cod and all work beautifully.*

EXTRA-HUNGRY KIDS? If you'd like to beef up the package with some potatoes, use canned ones. The fish and vegetables cook so fast that raw potatoes don't have a chance to get tender. Tender and flavorful, canned potatoes are a welcome addition for your hungrier tablemates.

ADULT TASTE BUDS? Add thinly sliced fennel, radishes, and/or chopped Kalamata olives and capers to adult portions before cooking.

IN THE GLASS: A light and racy white, such as a vinho verde from Portugal, has a little fizz and the light acidity to make this meal special.

Swordfish

with SWEET PEPPERS and GRILLED GARLIC BREAD

I lived in Spain back in the mid '70s in a little fishing village called La Carihuela. My travel buddy Anne and I would splurge on a nice piece of swordfish once a week from a little hut down the beach. The fisherman would saw a steak from the large fish lying on a wooden table and wrap it up in a piece of newspaper, and we'd carry it home to cook in our one and only pan with peppers, onions, and garlic in a puddle of fresh olive oil. Starving, we would gobble every last bite, sopping up all the juice on our plates with slices of toasted garlic bread. It was a feast fit for queens, or at least two starving twenty-year-olds on the adventure of their lives. Swordfish is such a dense, meaty fish that it's sometimes called the steak of the ocean. Its mild flavor allows a wide variety of possible seasonings and sides, and predictably, just about anything you like with a steak will go well with swordfish. But to me, there's nothing better than this simple Spanish taste memory.

5 garlic cloves	*¼ cup [60 ml] plus 3 Tbsp olive oil*
2 onions	*Kosher salt and freshly ground black pepper*
1 red bell pepper	*1 tsp paprika*
1 yellow bell pepper	*Four 6-oz [170-g] swordfish steaks, about 1 in [2.5 cm] thick*
1 green bell pepper	
2 large tomatoes	*2 tsp chopped fresh thyme*
	8 slices country-style bread

1. Preheat the grill to medium-high heat.

2. On a large cutting board, chop the garlic. Transfer it to a small bowl. Thinly slice the onions and bell peppers and transfer them to a medium bowl. Chop the tomatoes.

3. To make the garlic oil, heat a 12-in [30.5-cm] skillet over medium-high heat and add ¼ cup [60 ml] of the olive oil and half of the garlic. Heat until fragrant, about 2 minutes. Transfer to a heat-proof bowl.

4. Return the skillet to medium-high heat and add 2 Tbsp of the olive oil. When the oil shimmers, add the onions, bell peppers, and ¹/₂ tsp salt and sauté, stirring every now and then, until they soften, about 4 minutes. Add the paprika and the remaining garlic and stir for 1 minute, then add the tomatoes and cook until the juices evaporate and the mixture is jammy, about 3 minutes. Season with pepper and more salt if it needs it.

5. Pat the swordfish dry and season both sides with a sprinkle of salt, a few grinds of pepper, and thyme. Drizzle both sides with the remaining 1 Tbsp olive oil.

6. Grill the fish, turning once, just until cooked through, about 5 minutes on the first side and 3 or 4 minutes on the second side, depending on the thickness of the fish and heat of the grill. The fish should register 145°F [60°C] on an instant-read thermometer.

7. Meanwhile, brush the bread with the garlicky oil and sprinkle with salt and pepper. Grill the bread, oiled side down, until golden, 1 minute. Turn and toast the other side, another minute. Transfer to a platter.

8. Divide the swordfish steaks among heated plates and spoon the pepper mixture over the tops. Serve hot with the grilled bread.

It's that easy: *Swordfish is an excellent source of protein, potassium, selenium, and vitamins D and E, so it's not only good-tasting but good for you as well. It's also perfect for grilling just like—you guessed it—a steak.*

EXTRA-HUNGRY KIDS? Wrap canned sliced potatoes in foil packets with butter, salt and pepper, and a sprinkle of Parmesan cheese. Grill with the fish until warm.

 ADULT TASTE BUDS? Add chopped green olives and capers to the adult portions.

 IN THE GLASS: The vegetables here dictate a light red wine such as Pinot Noir. It can be hard to find a good inexpensive one, but La Crema Pinot Noir could be just the bottle you're looking for. The kids will appreciate a bubbly glass of cran-raspberry juice mixed with sparkling water.

START TO FINISH
30 minutes

HANDS-ON TIME
15 minutes

SERVES
4

Grouper with Swiss Chard,

TOMATOES, *and* FETA

Grouper is a favorite fish at our house. It's almost meaty in texture but it's still a mild and easy fish, enjoyed by adults and children alike. A chameleon, it also pairs well with just about any spice, herb, or vegetable, be it Indian, Mexican, Italian, or Asian. I've kept things really simple here with simmered greens and a little tomato and cheese, but feel free to gild the lily with a sprinkle of fish seasoning or any favorite ethnic herb blend currently in your spice drawer.

1 onion	*Kosher salt and freshly ground black pepper*
2 bunches Swiss chard	*2 Tbsp olive oil*
6 oz [170 g] grape tomatoes	*¹/₂ cup [60 g] crumbled feta cheese*
2 garlic cloves	*¹/₂ cup [120 ml] orange juice, apple juice, cranberry juice, or chicken or vegetable broth*
1¹/₂ lb [680 g] grouper, or another firm-fleshed fish, such as mahi-mahi or halibut, cut into 4 pieces	*2 Tbsp minced fresh parsley*

1. On a large cutting board, chop the onion; transfer to a medium bowl. Cut away the Swiss chard stems, chop them, and add them to the onion. Chop the chard leaves and transfer them to another bowl. Halve the tomatoes and mince the garlic into separate piles.

2. Season the grouper with salt and a few grinds of pepper.

3. Heat a 12-in [30.5-cm] skillet over medium-high heat and add the olive oil. When the oil shimmers,

add the onion and the chopped stems and sauté until they begin to soften, about 2 minutes. Add the garlic and a few handfuls of the leaves, adding the rest as they wilt, tossing and turning them with tongs. Season the greens with ¹/₄ tsp salt and a few grinds of pepper.

4. Scatter the tomatoes and feta over the top of the wilted greens and pour in the juice. Top the vegetables with the seasoned fish, cover, and reduce the heat to medium-low. Simmer until the fish is cooked through, 10 to 12 minutes. It should flake when pulled apart with a fork.

5. Divide the fish and vegetables among heated plates, sprinkle with the parsley, and serve.

It's that easy: *Don't like Swiss chard? Chop up a large head of escarole instead. Crazy about spinach? Cook up 20 oz [570 g] of baby spinach before laying the fish on top.*

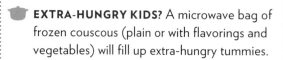

EXTRA-HUNGRY KIDS? A microwave bag of frozen couscous (plain or with flavorings and vegetables) will fill up extra-hungry tummies.

ADULT TASTE BUDS? Sprinkle the tops of the adult portions with garam masala (an Indian spice blend of cinnamon, cloves, nutmeg, pepper, and cardamom).

IN THE GLASS: A New Zealand Sauvignon Blanc from Whitehaven makes this weeknight meal feel like the weekend. If you are using orange juice in the recipe, a glass of orange juice mixed with coconut water is a refreshing option for the kids. You can do the same with apple or cranberry juice too.

Grouper with Artichokes,

NEW POTATOES, *and* PESTO DRIZZLE

Lean and firm-fleshed grouper is a member of the sea bass family. It can be cooked any number of ways, but its real claim to fame is its ability to pair with sauces and sides, making it the perfect fish for this pesto drizzle. Jars of marinated artichokes and roasted bell pepper add zip and color to the potatoes, making this dish way easier to assemble than it looks (shhh, don't tell anyone).

1 lb [455 g] new potatoes	*One 12-oz [340-g] jar marinated quartered artichokes*
1 onion	*¹/3 cup [10 g] grated Parmesan cheese*
1 garlic clove	*¹/3 cup [75 g] prepared pesto*
1 Tbsp olive oil	*1¹/2 lb [680 g] grouper, cut into 4 pieces*
Kosher salt and freshly ground black pepper	*4 oz [115 g] jarred chopped roasted red peppers, drained*

1. Line a sheet pan with aluminum foil and place it in the oven. Preheat the oven to 425°F [220°C].

2. On a large cutting board, thinly slice the potatoes (do not peel) and chop the onion and garlic. Transfer to a large bowl and toss with the olive oil, ¹/2 tsp salt, and a few grinds of pepper.

3. Remove the sheet pan from the oven and arrange the potato mixture evenly on the hot pan. Roast for 15 minutes.

4. While the potatoes roast, drain the jar of artichokes, reserving ¹/4 cup [60 ml] of the liquid in a

medium bowl. Add the Parmesan and pesto to the liquid and stir to combine. Set it aside.

5. Season the grouper with salt and pepper.

6. Remove the pan from the oven and scatter the artichokes and drained roasted peppers over the potatoes. Make space for the fish directly on the pan and roast until the fish flakes when checked with a fork and the potatoes are tender, about 15 minutes.

7. Divide the fish and vegetables among heated plates and drizzle with the pesto sauce. Serve hot.

continued

It's that easy: *Pesto is sold in a few different forms. You can buy it jarred on the grocery shelf but the refrigerated tubs are a better quality and color. The jarred versions can be kind of gray but they do taste okay. I guess I'm saying that if you can't find refrigerated pesto, it's fine to buy the jar, but if you can find the refrigerated version, buy that.*

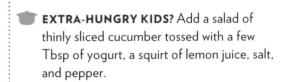 **EXTRA-HUNGRY KIDS?** Add a salad of thinly sliced cucumber tossed with a few Tbsp of yogurt, a squirt of lemon juice, salt, and pepper.

ADULT TASTE BUDS? Add caperberries, which are large capers, with the artichokes and peppers.

IN THE GLASS: When you're not sure what to drink with seafood, Sancerre is a good bet. A nice bottle for weeknight quaffing is Les Cailottes Sancerre.

Gratin of Haddock

with TOMATO and ZUCCHINI

I fell in love with haddock while vacationing in Maine a few years ago. It seems like others have fallen for it as well, becuase I now often spy it in my local Midwestern grocery. This homey gratin starts out with a little potato and then adds layers of grated zucchini, a touch of cream, haddock, tomato, and a buttery panko topping. Simple, delicious, and fast, this is a recipe for supper success.

6 new potatoes	*²/3 cup [40 g] panko bread crumbs*
2 garlic cloves	*1 Tbsp unsalted butter, melted*
2 Tbsp olive oil	*1½ lb [680 g] haddock, cut into 4 pieces*
Kosher salt and freshly ground black pepper	*1 tsp Italian seasoning*
3 zucchini	*¼ cup [60 ml] heavy cream*
1 tomato	

1. Preheat the oven to 425°F [220°C].

2. On a large cutting board, halve and thinly slice the potatoes (do not peel) and mince the garlic.

3. Heat a 12-in [30.5-cm] ovenproof skillet over medium-high heat and add the olive oil. When the oil shimmers, add the potatoes, garlic, ¼ tsp salt, and a few grinds of pepper. Stir to mix well and sauté until the potatoes are good and hot, about 3 minutes. Transfer the skillet to the oven and roast the potatoes for 10 minutes.

4. While the potatoes cook, grate the zucchini into a medium bowl and slice the tomato into eight slices.

5. In a small bowl, combine the panko and butter. Sprinkle the haddock with salt and a few grinds of pepper.

6. Remove the skillet from the oven (careful; the handle is hot) and stir in the zucchini, Italian seasoning, ¼ tsp salt, and a few grinds of pepper. Stir to mix well and cook over medium-high heat until hot, about 3 minutes. Lay the seasoned fish on top and then layer the tomatoes on top of the fish along with another sprinkle of salt and pepper. Pour the

continued

GO FISH

185

cream into the pan in a couple of spots so that it doesn't wash the seasoning off the fish and sprinkle the panko mixture over the tomatoes.

7. Return the skillet to the oven and cook until the fish flakes when checked with a fork and the topping is golden, about 15 minutes. Divide the gratin among heated plates and serve hot.

It's that easy: *If you can't find haddock, go ahead and use cod, tilapia, or any other firm-fleshed white fish. It will taste amazing.*

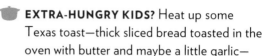

EXTRA-HUNGRY KIDS? Heat up some Texas toast—thick sliced bread toasted in the oven with butter and maybe a little garlic—and serve the vegetables and fish on top.

ADULT TASTE BUDS? Spread half the buttered panko over half the gratin, then mix 1 Tbsp prepared horseradish with the remaining panko mixture and spread over the adult portions.

IN THE GLASS: Your favorite Chardonnay is a great choice for this rich meal. If you haven't tried an unoaked Chardonnay, this is a good time to pick up a bottle from Kim Crawford or Estancia.

Coconut-Crusted Tilapia

with BROCCOLI and SWEET CHILI SAUCE

When we were kids, my siblings and I loved the coconut coating on coconut fried shrimp. We used to order it in this little Chinese place in Wheeling, West Virginia, where our parents took us for special occasions. You know in the movie *My Cousin Vinny* when Marisa Tomei makes the statement "I bet they have really bad Chinese here"? It was pretty much that place, but we loved it. I can still taste that crispy coconut coating doused in Chinese sauce. This is my homage to that memory, a slightly less sweet crusted fish with broccoli and the same sweet sauce.

1 bunch broccoli	*1½ lb [680 g] tilapia fillets*
1 shallot	*Kosher salt and freshly ground black pepper*
1 egg	*2 Tbsp vegetable oil*
1 cup [85 g] shredded unsweetened coconut	*¼ cup [60 ml] orange juice*
⅓ cup [45 g] all-purpose flour	*Sweet chili sauce*

1. Preheat the oven to 425°F [220°C].

2. On a large cutting board, trim the broccoli and cut it into long, thin spears, no more than ½ in [12 mm] thick. Cut the shallot in half lengthwise and then cut into ½-in [12-mm] slices. In a wide, shallow bowl, beat the egg with a fork. Pour the coconut and flour onto two separate plates.

3. Sprinkle the tilapia fillets with salt and a few grinds of pepper. Dredge the fillets in the flour, shaking off the excess, then dip them into the egg wash and dredge them in the coconut, patting the coconut on so that it adheres.

4. Heat a 12-in [30.5-cm] ovenproof skillet over medium-high heat and add the vegetable oil. When the oil shimmers, add the fish to the pan (don't crowd the pan; it may take two batches) and brown it on all sides, about 2 minutes per side. Transfer the fish to a plate. It will not be cooked through at this point.

5. Add the shallot and broccoli to the hot pan, along with a sprinkle of salt and pepper, and sauté for 2 minutes to get the cooking started. Add the orange juice and bring to a boil, then top with the fish. Transfer the skillet to the oven and roast until the fish is cooked through (it should flake when pulled apart with a fork) and the broccoli is tender, about 10 minutes.

6. Divide the fish and vegetables among heated plates and drizzle with the pan juices and sweet chili sauce.

It's that easy: *Sweet chili sauce isn't spicy. It's mostly sweet with a little Asian flair. The color is beautiful and it's great to have on hand to add to vinaigrettes, dipping sauces, and any place you'd like a touch of sugar. Keep the bottle in the fridge and it will last for a year or more. But I think you'll use it up sooner than that.*

EXTRA-HUNGRY KIDS? Add a can of drained sliced water chestnuts and a can of drained bamboo shoots along with the broccoli.

ADULT TASTE BUDS? Skip the sweet chili sauce and drizzle adult plates with a mixture of 2 Tbsp lime juice, 2 tsp soy sauce, 1 tsp Asian sesame oil, and 1/2 tsp chili garlic sauce or Sriracha.

IN THE GLASS: Trimbach Gewürztraminer from Alsace is the real deal. With a nice balance of minerality and notes of guava and white pepper, this wine will partner up with the sweeter notes in the dish. Blend guava nectar, coconut water, and sparkling water to make a breezy drink for the kids.

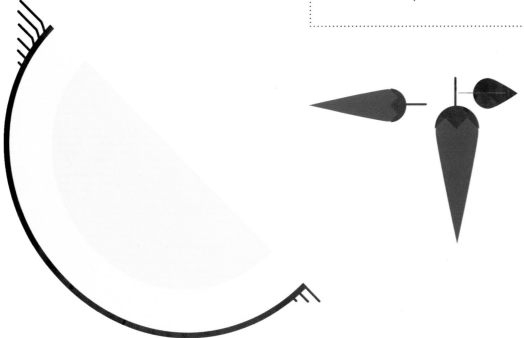

START TO FINISH
45 minutes
. . .
HANDS-ON TIME
25 minutes
. . .
SERVES
4

Cod Provençal

with POTATO CAKE

A crispy browned potato cake is a thing of beauty. A crispy browned potato cake topped with tomatoey fish with capers and olives is my idea of a happy meal . . . minus the Golden Arches, of course. You're going to love learning the technique of making the potato cake. If you don't already have one, buy an inexpensive plastic mandoline to slice the potatoes. It's an amazing time-saver and you'll use it to make dinner more than you would ever guess.

1 lb [455 g] red potatoes	8 pitted Kalamata olives
2 tsp unsalted butter	1 Tbsp capers
1 tsp olive oil	1 garlic clove
Kosher salt and freshly ground black pepper	1½ lb [680 g] cod, cut into 4 pieces
2 tomatoes	2 Tbsp chopped fresh basil

1. Slice the potatoes as thinly as possible on a mandoline, in a food processor using a slicing blade, or with a very sharp knife (do not peel).

2. Heat a 12-in [30.5-cm] nonstick skillet over medium heat and add the butter and olive oil. When the butter melts, quickly layer the potatoes in the skillet, slightly overlapping the slices, until the bottom of the pan is covered. Sprinkle with a tiny bit of salt and a few grinds of pepper and add another layer of potatoes, layering them in the opposite direction with a sprinkle of salt and a few grinds of pepper. Continue to lay down the potatoes in opposing directions (this keeps the cake from sliding apart once unmolded) until you've used all the potatoes.

3. The bottom of the pan should be crackling. Check the bottom of the potato cake, using a fork to pull it slightly up and away from the side of the pan to check how things are going; if lightly browned, cover, reduce the heat to low, and cook for about 15 minutes, checking every 5 minutes or so to make sure the bottom doesn't overbrown. If the cake is browning too quickly, reduce the heat and monitor the cooking closely. The potato cake is done when the sharp tip of a knife easily pierces the center of the cake.

4. While the potato cake cooks, on a large cutting board, chop the tomatoes, olives, capers, and garlic; transfer it all to a medium bowl. Sprinkle the cod with ½ tsp salt and a few grinds of pepper.

5. Invert a large plate over the top of the pan and carefully tilt the pan over a heatproof cup to pour out any extra oil in the pan. Flip the pan upside down to release the potato cake onto the plate. (I know it's hot. Use hot pads.) You should have a beautifully browned and tender potato cake. Cover it to keep warm. Return the pan to medium-high heat and add some of the oil back to the pan. Add the fish, tomato mixture, a sprinkle of salt, and a grind of pepper and bring to a simmer. Cover, reduce the heat to medium-low, and cook until the fish flakes when checked with a fork, about 7 minutes.

6. Cut the potato cake into four wedges and place in the center of heated plates. Top the wedges with the fish and vegetables, sprinkle with the basil, and serve.

It's that easy: *Back in cooking school, we used to call these potato cakes galettes. They are one of those classic French dishes that are crazy tasty because they are so crazy simple—nothing but potatoes, butter, oil, salt, and pepper. It's all about the technique of cooking at just the right heat so that the bottom of the cake browns and cooks through to tenderness, but not so hot that the bottom overbrowns and burns.*

EXTRA-HUNGRY KIDS? Add a salad of leaf lettuce, apples, carrots, a splash of cider vinegar, and a glug of olive oil.

ADULT TASTE BUDS? Top the adults' fish portions with a salad of shaved fennel tossed with a splash of lemon juice, a glug of olive oil, and a chopped anchovy.

IN THE GLASS: I love a glass of Côtes du Rhône with tomatoey fish. Look for a bottle of Guigal Côtes du Rhône for a medium-bodied red with nice fruit and enough acid to balance out the tomatoes in the dish.

PROSCIUTTO-ROASTED

Ruby Trout

with ZUCCHINI and BUTTER BEANS

Ruby trout is one of the most healthful of farmed fish because it's high in vitamin B_{12} and omega-3 fatty acids. Good-for-you is great, but the delicious taste is what makes ruby trout a perfect fish for family dinners. I've added a prosciutto wrapping to help keep the fish moist as it roasts with fresh zucchini, protein-packed butter beans, and zippy sun-dried tomatoes for a sheet-pan dinner that satisfies taste buds as well as growing bodies.

1 lb [455 g] zucchini

1 small red onion

2 garlic cloves

1 Tbsp olive oil

Kosher salt and freshly ground black pepper

4 thin slices prosciutto

1½ lb [680 g] ruby trout, cut into 4 fillets

One 15-oz [425-g] can butter beans, drained and rinsed

⅓ cup [20 g] julienned sun-dried tomatoes packed in oil

2 Tbsp minced fresh flat-leaf parsley

1. Line a sheet pan with aluminum foil and place it in the oven. Preheat the oven to 425°F [220°C].

2. On a large cutting board, halve the zucchini lengthwise and slice thinly; transfer to a large bowl. Slice the onion and chop the garlic and add them to the zucchini. Add the olive oil, ½ tsp salt, and a few grinds of pepper and toss to mix well.

3. Remove the sheet pan from the oven and arrange the vegetables evenly on the hot pan. Roast for 15 minutes.

4. While the vegetables roast, cut the prosciutto in half lengthwise to make eight long strips.

5. Season the trout with salt (not too much, as the prosciutto is salty) and a few grinds of pepper, and wrap each fillet with two strips of prosciutto. Don't worry if it doesn't stick; it will adhere very nicely after cooking.

6. In a medium bowl, combine the butter beans and sun-dried tomatoes with a sprinkle of salt and a few grinds of pepper.

7. Remove the sheet pan from the oven, push the vegetables to one side of the pan, and arrange the trout evenly on the other side. Scatter the butter bean mixture over the vegetables and cook until the

continued

fish flakes with a fork and the beans are hot, about 10 minutes.

8. Divide the vegetables and fish among heated plates and sprinkle with the parsley. Serve hot.

It's that easy: *If you don't like fish skin, you can ask your fishmonger to remove it for you or just lay the prosciutto on top of the fish so you can easily pull the skin off after it's cooked.*

 **EXTRA-HUNGRY KIDS?** Add an extra zucchini or, better yet, a yellow summer squash for color. More veggies, more better.

ADULT TASTE BUDS? Spread the adult portions of fish with 2 tsp Dijon mustard before wrapping in prosciutto for added spice and moisture.

IN THE GLASS: This ruby-hued fish is similar in taste to salmon or arctic char so the same white wine applies . . . Chardonnay. Look for a nice bottle from Dry Creek Vineyard. Pink fish and a pink drink will make the kids smile. Combine strawberry juice with sparkling water and garnish with a lemon slice.

Asian-Style Fish Tacos

with WILTED CABBAGE SLAW

Sautéed fish tacos are just as delicious as fried; plus, they're faster and easier to get on the table on a busy weeknight. I'm really into the toppings on tacos, and this warm slaw with Asian flavors is one of my favorites. Rice vinegar, soy sauce, honey, and sesame oil season bagged slaw to a T and the zippy lime mayo and avocado add richness and depth to what might be my favorite dinner in the book. I've kept it simple here, but feel free to add pickled red onions, jalapeños, and sliced bell peppers to jazz it up if you have the time.

2 ripe avocados	2 Tbsp vegetable oil
¼ cup [10 g] fresh cilantro	1½ Tbsp soy sauce
2 green onions	1 Tbsp honey
1 garlic clove	2 tsp Asian sesame oil
2 limes	⅓ cup [80 g] mayonnaise
1 lb [455 g] tilapia, snapper, catfish, or other white fish	8 oz [230 g] packaged coleslaw mix
Kosher salt and freshly ground black pepper	8 to 12 corn tortillas
2 Tbsp unseasoned rice vinegar	Roasted peanuts

1. On a large cutting board, peel, pit, and slice the avocado; transfer it to a small plate. Chop the cilantro and slice the green onions and transfer them to a medium bowl. Mince the garlic. Halve one lime and quarter the other. Cut the fish into pieces about 4 in [10 cm] long and season them with salt and a few grinds of pepper.

2. Combine the vinegar, 1 Tbsp of the vegetable oil, the soy sauce, honey, and sesame oil in a small bowl.

3. Combine the mayonnaise and the juice from one lime half in another small bowl.

4. Heat a 12-in [30.5-cm] skillet over medium-high heat and add the remaining 1 Tbsp vegetable oil. When the oil shimmers, add the seasoned fish to the pan in batches, being careful not to overcrowd the pan. Cook the fish for 3 minutes, turn it over, and cook for another 3 minutes. As you work,

continued

GO FISH

transfer the cooked fish to a plate and keep warm while cooking the remaining fish.

5. Add the garlic to the hot pan and sauté until fragrant, about 30 seconds. Add the vinegar mixture to the pan and bring to a boil. Remove the pan from the heat and quickly add the coleslaw mix, stirring to combine it well. Immediately transfer the warmed slaw to the bowl with the cilantro and green onion, mixing well. Taste and squeeze in the remaining halved lime and a sprinkle of salt and pepper if it needs it.

6. Warm the tortillas on a plate, covered with microwave-safe plastic wrap, in the microwave for 30 seconds to 1 minute.

7. Serve the slaw, avocado, fish, tortillas, quartered lime, lime mayo, and peanuts at the table for the family to assemble their own tacos any way they like them.

It's that easy: *You can make pickled onions in no time. Combine 3 Tbsp red wine vinegar, 2 Tbsp water, 1 Tbsp sugar, and 1/2 tsp salt in a large microwave-safe measuring cup or bowl and microwave until the sugar is dissolved and the mixture is hot, about 2 minutes. Immediately add 1 small thinly sliced red onion and push it under the liquid. Let sit for 10 minutes and then use as you'd like. Keep refrigerated for up to 1 week.*

 EXTRA-HUNGRY KIDS? Double-wrap the tacos with two tortillas instead of just one.

 ADULT TASTE BUDS? Pickled onions, anyone? (See "It's that easy.")

 IN THE GLASS: I like beer with tacos, and just about any beer you want to drink will be terrific with the fish. Why not try something local you've never tried before? Any IPA will work beautifully. Make this meal a party for everyone and serve the kids nonalcoholic lime daiquiris, umbrellas optional.

Lemony Halibut

with FENNEL, GRAPE TOMATOES, *and* CARROTS

Halibut is one of the most delicious of fishes. Firm-fleshed, light, and mild, it's always popular at our house, and especially so when paired with colorful vegetables and a lemony vinaigrette. It's kind of like spa food at an expensive resort . . . only you get to eat it at home.

3 carrots	*Zest of 1/2 lemon*
1 large or 2 small fennel bulbs plus fronds	*2 Tbsp lemon juice*
10 oz [285 g] grape tomatoes	*1 tsp Dijon mustard*
1 shallot	*1 1/2 lb [680 g] halibut*
1/4 cup [60 ml] olive oil	*1/2 cup [60 g] frozen peas, thawed*
Kosher salt and freshly ground black pepper	*2 Tbsp chopped fresh parsley*

1. Line a sheet pan with aluminum foil and place it in the oven. Preheat the oven to 425°F [220°C].

2. On a large cutting board, peel and thinly slice the carrots. Thinly slice the fennel, mince 1 Tbsp of the fronds, and halve the tomatoes. As you work, transfer the vegetables to a large bowl. Mince the shallot and add half to the vegetables and half to a small bowl for the vinaigrette.

3. Toss the vegetables with 1 Tbsp of the olive oil, 1/2 tsp salt, and a few grinds of pepper. Arrange the vegetables on the hot sheet pan, spreading them out so that they cook evenly, and roast for 5 minutes.

4. While the vegetables roast, make the vinaigrette. Add the lemon zest, juice, mustard, and a sprinkle of salt and pepper to the bowl with the shallot. Let rest for 5 minutes to develop the flavors, then whisk in the remaining 3 Tbsp olive oil.

5. Season the fish with salt and pepper. Make space for it to rest directly on the sheet pan with the vegetables and drizzle the fish with 1 Tbsp vinaigrette. Roast for another 15 minutes, or until the fish is cooked through and flakes when pulled apart with a fork. Sprinkle the peas over the vegetables and return to the oven for 1 minute to heat.

continued

6. Divide the fish and vegetables among heated plates, drizzle the fish and vegetables with the remaining vinaigrette, and sprinkle with the parsley. Serve hot.

It's that easy: *Fennel is delicious thinly sliced in salads or roasted. It's usually found in the produce section with tall stalks and feathery fronds that look something like dill but with an anise-like flavor. I usually cut the stalks off and discard them, saving some of the fronds, then slice the bulb into quarters so I can easily cut away the core before slicing the bulb according to the recipe.*

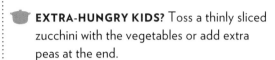 **EXTRA-HUNGRY KIDS?** Toss a thinly sliced zucchini with the vegetables or add extra peas at the end.

ADULT TASTE BUDS? For a spicy kick, toss the adult portions of vegetables with a few tsp harissa before roasting. It's a North African spice blend composed of cumin, paprika, chile peppers, garlic, coriander, and other herbs. It can appear as a paste or a powder and either way it adds an interesting edge to vegetables and meats.

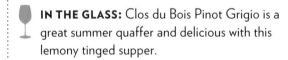 **IN THE GLASS:** Clos du Bois Pinot Grigio is a great summer quaffer and delicious with this lemony tinged supper.

find it fast

Spring Forward (Spring Meals)

- Pizza with Pesto, Grape Tomatoes, and Mozzarella, 19
- Cheesy Angel Hair Pasta with Asparagus and Basil, 29
- Spring Mushroom and Pea Risotto, 31
- Asian Brussels Sprouts with Brown Rice, 34
- Roasted Broccoli with Peanuts and Brown Rice, 36
- Parmesan-Crusted Cauliflower Steaks with Farro, 38
- Curry Roasted Carrots and Lentils with Orange-Yogurt Sauce, 48
- White Pizza with Fontina, Chicken, and Arugula, 59
- Orange Chicken Stew with Red Pepper and Sweet Potatoes, 66
- Drumsticks with Barbecue Glaze and Confetti Corn, 78
- Pasta Salad with Chicken, Grapes, and Walnuts, 82
- Chicken Saltimbocca with Broccolini and Couscous, 90
- Fried Chicken Tenders with Corn Cakes and Honey, 95
- Stracciatella with Chicken and Croutons, 104
- Chicken Soup with Black Beans, Corn, and Pepitas, 106
- Chicken Soup with Leeks and Wide Noodles, 109
- Tortilla Soup with Chicken and Sausage, 111
- Tomato Pizza with Spinach, Fresh Mozzarella, and Pepperoni, 116
- Bacon Frittata with Broccoli, Red Bell Pepper, and Cheddar, 118
- Rosemary Pork Tenderloin with Carrots and Fig-Yogurt Sauce, 133
- Flat Iron Steak with Broccoli Slaw, 146
- Beef Kebabs with Zucchini and Tomatoes, 148
- Thai Steak Salad, 151
- Beef Fajitas with Guacamole, 153
- Shrimp Pizza with Pineapple and Spinach, 168

- Red Curry Shrimp, 170
- Bow Ties with Shrimp, Spinach, and Feta, 173
- Swordfish with Sweet Peppers and Grilled Garlic Bread, 178
- Grouper with Artichokes, New Potatoes, and Pesto Drizzle, 183
- Coconut-Crusted Tilapia with Broccoli and Sweet Chili Sauce, 188
- Asian-Style Fish Tacos with Wilted Cabbage Slaw, 195
- Lemony Halibut with Fennel, Grape Tomatoes and Carrots, 198

Hot Town Summer in the City (Summer Meals)

- Pizza with Pesto, Grape Tomatoes, and Mozzarella, 19
- Cheesy Angel Hair Pasta with Asparagus and Basil, 29
- Roasted Broccoli with Peanuts and Brown Rice, 34
- Roasted Vegetable, Feta, and Smoked Almond Salad, 43
- White Pizza with Fontina, Chicken, and Arugula, 59
- Chicken Thighs with Balsamic Barbecue Sauce and Corn on the Cob, 73
- Chicken Sliders with Chipotle Slaw, 76
- Drumsticks with Barbecue Glaze and Confetti Corn, 78
- Pasta Salad with Chicken, Grapes, and Walnuts, 82
- Chicken Saltimbocca with Broccolini and Couscous, 90
- Tomato Pizza with Spinach, Fresh Mozzarella, and Pepperoni, 116
- Bacon Frittata with Broccoli, Red Bell Pepper, and Cheddar, 118
- Rosemary Pork Tenderloin with Carrots and Fig-Yogurt Sauce, 133
- Sausage and Pepper Hoagies with Red Sauce, 138
- Flat Iron Steak with Broccoli Slaw, 146
- Beef Kebabs with Zucchini and Tomatoes, 148
- Thai Steak Salad, 151
- Beef Fajitas with Guacamole, 153
- Open-Faced Super Burgers with Cheddar, Mushrooms, and Onion, 156

- Shrimp Pizza with Pineapple and Spinach, 168
- Red Curry Shrimp, 170
- Bow Ties with Shrimp, Spinach, and Feta, 173
- Snapper Papillote with Summer Vegetables and Herb Butter, 175
- Swordfish with Sweet Peppers and Grilled Garlic Bread, 178
- Grouper with Swiss Chard, Tomatoes, and Feta, 180
- Coconut-Crusted Tilapia with Broccoli and Sweet Chili Sauce, 188
- Prosciutto-Roasted Ruby Trout with Zucchini and Butter Beans, 193
- Asian-Style Fish Tacos with Wilted Cabbage Slaw, 195
- Lemony Halibut with Fennel, Grape Tomatoes and Carrots, 198

Falling Leaves (Autumn Meals)

- Pimiento Grilled Cheese Sandwiches, 21
- Potato Casserole with Swiss Chard, 24
- Sweet Potato Gratin with Spinach, 26
- Asian Brussels Sprouts with Brown Rice, 34
- Roasted Broccoli with Peanuts and Brown Rice, 36
- Parmesan-Crusted Cauliflower Steaks with Farro, 38
- Roasted Vegetable, Feta, and Smoked Almond Salad, 43
- Roasted Beet Salad with Oranges, Goat Cheese, and Walnuts, 46
- Curry Roasted Carrots and Lentils with Orange-Yogurt Sauce, 48
- Vegetable Soup with Poached Eggs, 50
- Curried Lentil Soup, 52
- Sweet Potato Soup with Apple-y Cheese Quesadilla, 54
- Deviled Roast Chicken with Bacon and Brussels Sprout Hash, 61
- Orange Chicken Stew with Red Pepper and Sweet Potatoes, 66
- Chicken Thighs with Sausage, Red Beans, and Rice, 68
- Chicken and Swiss Chard in Cider-Cream Sauce, 71
- Honey-Chipotle Chicken with Root Vegetables, 80

Baby It's Cold Outside (Winter Meals)

Dairy Free

- Asian Brussels Sprouts with Brown Rice, 34
- Roasted Broccoli with Peanuts and Brown Rice, 36
- Root Vegetable Quinoa Bowl with Tahini, 41
- Vegetable Soup with Poached Eggs, 50
- Curried Lentil Soup, 52
- Deviled Roast Chicken with Bacon and Brussels Sprout Hash, 61
- Cuban-Style Chicken Fricassee, 64
- Orange Chicken Stew with Red Pepper and Sweet Potatoes, 66
- Chicken Thighs with Sausage, Red Beans, and Rice, 68
- Chicken Thighs with Balsamic Barbecue Sauce and Corn on the Cob, 73
- Chicken Sliders with Chipotle Slaw, 76
- Drumsticks with Barbecue Glaze and Confetti Corn, 78
- Honey-Chipotle Chicken with Root Vegetables, 80
- Tandoori Chicken with Spiced Cauliflower, 85
- Tuscan Chicken with Sun-Dried Tomatoes and Mushrooms, 87
- Chicken Saltimbocca with Broccolini and Couscous, 90
- Sweet-and-Sour Turkey Meatballs with Brown Rice, 100
- Turkey Chili with Chiles and Black Beans, 102
- Stracciatella with Chicken and Croutons, 104
- Chicken Soup with Black Beans, Corn, and Pepitas, 106
- Chicken Soup with Leeks and Wide Noodles, 109
- Tortilla Soup with Chicken and Sausage, 111
- Ribollita with Ham, 120
- Pork Chops with Sweet Potatoes and Apple Glaze, 130
- Italian Sausage with Cabbage and Lentils, 135
- Sausage and Pepper Hoagies with Red Sauce, 138
- Italian Sausage with Grape Tomatoes and Polenta, 140

- Butter Bean Stew with Kielbasa, 142
- Kielbasa with Sauerkraut, Apple, and Vegetables, 144
- Flat Iron Steak with Broccoli Slaw, 146
- Beef Kebabs with Zucchini and Tomatoes, 148
- Thai Steak Salad, 151
- Beef Fajitas with Guacamole, 153
- Red Curry Shrimp, 170
- Swordfish with Sweet Peppers and Grilled Garlic Bread, 178
- Grouper with Artichokes, New Potatoes, and Pesto Drizzle, 183
- Cod Provençal with Potato Cake, 190
- Prosciutto-Roasted Ruby Trout with Zucchini and Butter Beans, 193
- Asian-Style Fish Tacos with Wilted Cabbage Slaw, 195
- Lemony Halibut with Fennel, Grape Tomatoes and Carrots, 198

Gluten Free

- Potato Casserole with Swiss Chard, 24
- Sweet Potato Gratin with Spinach, 26
- Spring Mushroom and Pea Risotto, 31
- Asian Brussels Sprouts with Brown Rice, 34
- Roasted Broccoli with Peanuts and Brown Rice, 36
- Root Vegetable Quinoa Bowl with Tahini, 41
- Roasted Vegetable, Feta, and Smoked Almond Salad, 43
- Roasted Beet Salad with Oranges, Goat Cheese, and Walnuts, 46
- Curry Roasted Carrots and Lentils with Orange-Yogurt Sauce, 48
- Vegetable Soup with Poached Eggs, 50
- Curried Lentil Soup, 52
- Deviled Roast Chicken with Bacon and Brussels Sprout Hash, 61
- Cuban-Style Chicken Fricassee, 64
- Orange Chicken Stew with Red Pepper and Sweet Potatoes, 66
- Chicken Thighs with Sausage, Red Beans, and Rice, 68
- Chicken and Swiss Chard in Cider-Cream Sauce, 71
- Chicken Thighs with Balsamic Barbecue Sauce and Corn on the Cob, 73

- Drumsticks with Barbecue Glaze and Confetti Corn, 78
- Honey-Chipotle Chicken with Root Vegetables, 80
- Tandoori Chicken with Spiced Cauliflower, 85
- Tuscan Chicken with Sun-Dried Tomatoes and Mushrooms, 87
- Sweet-and-Sour Turkey Meatballs with Brown Rice, 100
- Turkey Chili with Chiles and Black Beans, 102
- Chicken Soup with Black Beans, Corn, and Pepitas, 106
- Tortilla Soup with Chicken and Sausage, 111
- Bacon Frittata with Broccoli, Red Bell Pepper, and Cheddar, 118
- Ribollita with Ham, 120
- Pork Chops with Sweet Potatoes and Apple Glaze, 130
- Rosemary Pork Tenderloin with Carrots and Fig-Yogurt Sauce, 133
- Italian Sausage with Cabbage and Lentils, 135
- Italian Sausage with Grape Tomatoes and Polenta, 140
- Butter Bean Stew with Kielbasa, 142
- Kielbasa with Sauerkraut, Apple, and Vegetables, 144
- Flat Iron Steak with Broccoli Slaw, 146
- Beef Kebabs with Zucchini and Tomatoes, 148
- Thai Steak Salad, 151
- Barbecue Meat Loaf Patties with Herbed Smashed Potatoes and Green Beans, 158
- Red Curry Shrimp, 170
- Snapper Papillote with Summer Vegetables and Herb Butter, 175
- Grouper with Swiss Chard, Tomatoes, and Feta, 180
- Grouper with Artichokes, New Potatoes, and Pesto Drizzle, 183
- Prosciutto-Roasted Ruby Trout with Zucchini and Butter Beans, 193
- Lemony Halibut with Fennel, Grape Tomatoes and Carrots, 198

index

Acknowledgments

Thank you to the extraordinary people at Chronicle Books for creating the most beautiful cookbooks in the business. I send much affection and gratitude to my editor par excellence, Amy Treadwell, for her vision, expert eye, and unerring advice, to managing editors Marie Oishi and Margo Winton Parodi for polishing the manuscript till it sparkled, and to copyeditor Cheryl Redmond for her tireless attention to detail. *Mille mercis* to art director Alice Chau, designer Cat Grishaver, photographer Colin Price, prop stylist Glenn Jenkins, and food stylist Emily Caneer for the gorgeous photography and design creating a timeless, easy-to-read book to be proud of for many years to come. Kudos to senior production developer Tera Killip and marketing manager Alexandra Brown for putting ink to paper and for packaging and promoting *One Pan, Whole Family* to the masses.

With appreciation to my countless students, friends, and family who've recipe tested and critiqued over the years: Julie Neri, Mary Lohman, Sarah McNally, Brigitte Gottfried, Anne Pitkin, Tammy Karasek, Sarina Kinney, Maria Isabella, Anne Gallagher, Janet Redman, Jan Prengaman, Alicia Ravens, Patricia Rose, Jamie Stevens, Lyndsey Snyder, Zona Spray, Mary Lohman, Taylor Horen, Vikki Watkins, Nick Caringi and the Caringi family, Matt and Lisa Meyers, Suzie Mayer, Bridget Walland, Claudia Codispoti, Patti Hermsen, Suzie Mayer, Angela and Terry Gagel, Connie Sandberg, Sue Gumbart, and Sue Abledinger. I hope you've found some new family dinner favorites. You guys are the best.

Special thanks to my kids Jessica, Justin, and Corey, daughters-in-law, Lyndsey and Sara, and son-in-law JR for bartending, prepping, cooking, dish washing, and generally entertaining us all at family dinners and get-togethers. You are my favorite people in the world. And to my beautiful grandbabies Kyley, Emma, Charlie, and the new one who hasn't quite arrived yet, for making me smile and always, always keeping me moving.

And last but not least, thanks to my darling husband, Rick, for 40 years of support, friendship, and humor that enabled me to discover and develop a passion for creating recipes and writing about food. I never could have done it without you.